Amish
Gardening
Secrets

By Marcy D. Nicholas

Published by:

James Direct Inc.
500 S. Prospect Ave.
Hartville, Ohio 44632
U.S.A.

ISBN: 978-1-62397-030-7

Printing 12 11 10 9

First Edition   Copyright 2005   James Direct Inc.

Table of Contents

Laura's Thought for the Day...

Now faith is the substance of things hoped for, the evidence of things not seen. The Bible was telling me, Hope is faith relating to the future. Conviction is faith relating to the present.
Hebrew/ 11:1

Dedication

My sincere thanks to Laura Yoder whose time spent with me was invaluable in completing this project. Also thank you to Darlene for bringing me and Laura together. And to the two new angels who light up the sky, Fran and Bill – we will never forget you.

Chapter 1:

Amish Charm

As you follow the charming winding roads deep in the
heart of Amish country, you will come across the aptly
named town of Charm. Nestled within the hillside are
the Amish homes, farms and schools that make up this
community. And it is here where our story begins...

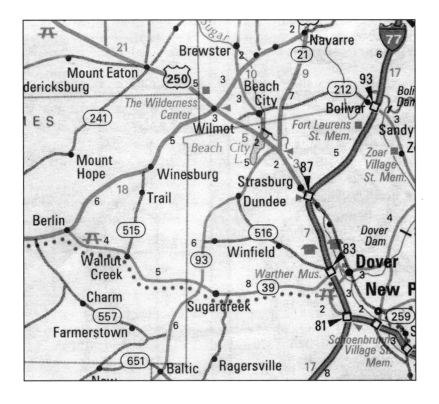

Charm is located in Holmes County and is part of the
largest Amish settlement in the world. Known as Holmes
County and vicinity in Northeastern Ohio, 30,000 or more -
one in every six Amish live here.

The second largest settlement, which is also the oldest
and most famous community is in Lancaster County in

Southeastern Pennsylvania where 18,000 Amish make their home. The other two large settlements are in the northern Indiana counties of Elkhart and LaGrange and 50 miles east of Cleveland, Ohio in Geauga County. A little known fact is that there are no Amish settlements remaining in Europe.

The Amish have captured the interest of the modern world because of their quaint clothing, homes and buggies, their striking quilts, their lusty food. These people prefer to be regarded as a community of faith who deliberately seek to live in a way that honors God and the creation. They purposely refuse many conveniences to better cultivate their life together. They choose to live close to the land in an effort to care for their families and the earth.

Laura Yoder has lived most of her life here in Charm, having grown up in nearby Mt. Hope. As I drive up to her home and park my car, Laura gives me a smile and a wave. Hoe in hand, she continues to tend to her garden while I gather my things and make my way to her door. On an Amish homestead, there is no such thing as wasting time.

A small woman, Laura has a quick smile and intelligent eyes. While she may be small, I would venture to guess that she could out arm wrestle me! As she leads the way upstairs on this particular morning, I see glistening jars of freshly canned green beans adorning the table in her canning kitchen. As I admire these I remember that Laura starts her day at 4:30 AM.

Note: Although many people have been kind enough to share their remedies, recipes and gardening secrets in this book, it is Laura's words that you will see featured throughout these pages.

Chapter 2:

Amish History and Traditions

The Amish are a different group from the Mennonites, but they share the same roots. Both groups are variations of Christianity and both are part of a branch of Protestantism that is known as Anabaptism. The Anabaptist movement began in 1525 and emphasized the importance of adult baptism.

The Amish started in 1693 and split from the Mennonites because they felt they had become too worldly. Most Mennonites use electricity, own and drive cars and wear traditional clothes.

In 1913, the group known today as the Swartzentruber Amish broke away from the Old Order because they believed the group was too progressive.

Events that occurred on November 19, 1965 and May 15, 1972 near Hazelton, Iowa resulted in a change in the law regarding Amish education. For years and years the Amish resisted compulsory state mandated education. On these particular dates a group of Amish children hid in a cornfield to avoid being bussed to a public school. The end result was a Supreme Court exemption for the Amish thereby allowing them to have their own schools without the state's interference. Today most Amish children attend parochial schools supported by Amish congregations.

The Amish do not believe in collecting social security upon retirement. So in 1965 Congress granted the Amish an exemption from paying social security taxes as a rider to a Medicare bill. This applied except in the instance when they are working for a non-Amish employer.

In 1990, the US Supreme Court overturned a Minnesota State Supreme Court decision which required the Amish to place slow moving vehicle (SMV) signs on the back of their buggies. Other states continue to pursue legislation requiring these SMV's on buggies. Most Amish use them except those who belong to the most conservative affiliations. Other disagreements between Amish and government regulations continue to this day such as wearing orange when hunting, health regulations on septic systems as well as safety regulations in Amish owned sawmills and other businesses.

Prohibition on the use of electricity and phones goes back to the early 1900's. However, the Amish have compromised on the use of the telephone. Many "telephone shanties" can be found on the back roads in areas where the Amish live. They are usually located at the end of a lane or across the street from the home. The phone is owned by Amish, and the number is usually unlisted. The phone's use is restricted to making appointments and conducting business with non-Amish. The phones are often equipped with voice mail to enable Amish businesses to receive messages and return phone calls. Some Amish business owners even have cell phones.

The Amish don't permit use of electricity from public power lines but there are compromises here as well. The Amish will use batteries to start stationary engines, run adding machines, calculators, clocks, flashlights and other workshop and household items. Many Amish businesses use large diesel engines for lighting and to run hydraulic power tools and machinery. Gas-powered refrigerators and lights and compressed air powered water well pumps are also used in homes. The Amish also use solar powered batteries for lights on buggies, charged fencing for cows and ice cream makers. The more traditional Amish use wood-burning stoves to heat their homes while others rely on gas heat. Gas lamps are usually used for reading.

About 20 years ago new state regulations required that milk be kept cool in order to be sold on the market as Grade A. Almost all Amish farms have dairy cows and milk is a good source of regular income. This created hardship for Amish farms. An agreement worked out between Amish bishops and various local and state health agencies ruled that the bulk milk tanks be cooled with a diesel or gasoline generator. The milk tank agitator or stirrer can run off of 12 volt car batteries. If temperatures aren't sufficient for Grade A milk, Amish farmers have the option of selling it to businesses that make cheese.

Amish Laws

Ordnung (ott-nuing) The Amish live according to the rules of the *Ordnung*, an unwritten but specific prescription for behavior. These guidelines don't abolish convenience or disapprove of comfort but they embrace plainness, thrift and identity. The purpose of any prohibition is to safeguard their separateness from a society that the Amish consider worldly. It is a set of rules and regulations for living and a declaration of the Amish faith. There is never any striving for individual success and pleasure, rather the *Ordnung* draws boundaries to make it easier for the Amish to follow their community's Bible based aims. The Amish are organized into church districts each composed of several dozen families headed by a group of elders including a bishop, two ministers and one deacon. No formal training is necessary to become bishop, minister or deacon, they are chosen by lot. Each district has its own *ordnung*. That is why different groups of Amish do things differently. Some drive buggies that have no rearview mirrors, others have mirrors but paint the chrome around the mirror black while others don't paint the chrome at all. The Swartzentruber Amish doesn't allow glass anywhere on the buggy – no windshields, rearview mirrors, windows or turn signals. The only way to see what's behind you is to stick your head out and look back. Old Order Amish don't use inflated tires. While this may seem like a simple mode of transportation, on a bicycle a child could quickly get far from home – far away from the heart of Amish life. Using scooters and horse drawn carriages keep brakes on the distance the Amish can travel and supports home centered living. The *Ordnung* forbids air travel and driving a car. In all Amish church districts, the *ordnung* is constantly examined and adjusted. For the most part the *ordnung* is verbal and only a few parts of it are written down.

...There was just a lot of practices, courtship practices among the Amish youth that we didn't feel was Biblical so a lot of that has changed that it's more Biblical. I don't know why they started those practices. I have no idea, but among the youth there were a lot of practice that were not Biblical so that has changed a lot. I guess some groups still do have their parties. But there was parties that was not Biblical at a lot of that has changed and it is more into the Biblical and that's the ways it's stricter now then it was...

Meidung (mide-ung) is shunning. If a member of the church strays and refuses to confess he is shunned. They can't eat or do business with other members. Because of the isolating power of this ban, the Amish seriously fulfill their religious obligations. Only adults who have been baptized Amish are subject to the *meidung*. It is used almost exclusively for the punishment of sins not relating to the *ordnung*, but for sins as described in the Bible. Shunning is considered a last resort, the end result of a series of failed attempts at reconciliation with the *ordnung* of the church district. If the person sincerely repents, fellowship will again be restored. Disagreements about the use of *meidung* is one of the issues that caused the Amish to split off from the Mennonites in 1693. It has also contributed to several divisions within the Amish during this century.

Gelassenheit (gay-las-en-hite) means yielding to a higher authority. It represents expectations for the appropriate way to speak and to behave, such as not drawing attention to one's self through verbal boasting or non-conforming dress. It symbolizes a church of members in close knit fellowship, who continuously discuss issues of faith and ways they should lead their lives.

Amish Values

Sundays are free from all but necessary work to honor the Sabbath. So that is the day for visiting. One characteristic that distinguishes the Amish from almost all other denominations is that they conduct their church service in member's houses. The Sunday service rotates from one home to another. A typical district hosting a service means having 200 or more people coming to the house. It lasts about 3 1/2 hours. After church services, families gather to socialize. That is followed by a meal where people stay to talk and visit until it is time to go home for the late afternoon and evening chores.

The Amish believe that seeing each other and talking face to face is much better than talking on the telephone. For this reason, the Old Order Amish forbid having a phone in the house.

...We did a lot of visiting. My dad was a deacon when we

were a little bit older and they would always go off to church. That was kind of when it stopped that we didn't go visiting so much. We have church every other Sunday. On the in-between Sunday we would go visit other churches or go visit family. So those were always good days. And the Sundays that we didn't do that we would spend at home at Bible study and singing, which those were good days too. Now it's different. You don't just pack up and go and not tell people that you're coming, for us it's a big difference...

God was always at the center of life and centered around God was family.

... My mom passed away a year ago in February and we would always be at church or at mom's place because she couldn't go away. For about 15 years there was always somebody home, and it was about thirteen miles away. We don't want to start going someplace like that when you don't know if the people on the other end would be home so that's a big difference. Back then you would just go because there was always somebody there so that's a big difference in our family right now. So I guess we got old, we just love to stay home...

Family Life magazine promotes spiritual and plain living and reaches many Amish homes. Many subscribe to *Readers Digest, Farm Journal* and religious publications. Mainstream and Amish newspapers are the main source of news. The Amish highly regard learning, not for its own sake but for improving their income-generating skills and for deepening their spiritual understanding.

Illiteracy is virtually non-existent in their settlements. They learn by doing. The Amish are inclined to pursue inventions or systems that will solve a local problem. One young man devised equipment to make methane gas and organic compost from manure. Another invented a gauge to record the gas in a silo. This device saved many lives.

The Amish use modern medicine but normally visit a doctor only as a last resort. Money is often pooled to pay for medical expenses. The Amish eat a diet of whole foods and tend to use natural remedies for ailments that include food and herbal tonics.

Amish Dress

Women dress uniformly in solid colored fabric removing the competitiveness of fashion from their lives. All women, even little girls as young as six weeks old wear a covering on their head at all times. This is called a prayer covering. It is a symbol of submission to God and His structure of authority. It is worn until they die. Women both young and old wear an apron. Brides wear a white cape and apron and usually a blue dress. Single and married women wear a white cape and apron to church all of their lives. Colored capes and aprons are worn at most other functions and is usually the same color as the dress.

Boys at age four start wearing an adult-styled suit which includes a vest, suspenders, coat, hat and "broadfall" trousers. These have pockets only on the inside where they can't be considered decorative. Adult men grow beards with their hair cut straight not layered just below the ears. Sideburns are prohibited. Men shave until marriage. The beard serves in some ways in lieu of a wedding band. Men wear distinctive broad-brimmed hat (straw in summer) whenever they are outside the house. The more conservative the group, the wider the brim of the hat and the higher the crown. Conservative districts restrict themselves to darker clothes. More progressive districts allow lighter colors.

Amish Simplicity

The Amish choose to live with simplicity rather than clutter and luxury. The only pictures on the walls of their homes are small ones attached to calendars. They have the belief that adornment may lead into luxuries and unsuitable behavior. It is taboo to converse about new purchases or efforts at self improvement. The Amish value humility and meekness often to the point of speaking softly and slowly. This demeanor grows out of a deep belief that they are the servants of God living on earth to do God's will, not to promote themselves. It is for this reason that photography is not permitted. The Amish believe that it promotes pride and individualism.

Silence gathers people. The absence of radio, television,

telephone and home entertainment systems creates a quiet environment that allows a family to talk, joke, read or play table games. A regular silent prayer during the church service draws the community into humility before God.

Pennsylvania Dutch or German is the language spoken at home by the Amish. It helps them maintain their distinctiveness. The language reminds them of their origins from German speaking areas of Europe, and it reminds them that they are a separate people who follow their particular way to observe their Christian faith. It is the language of work, family, friendship, play and intimacy. An Amish version of standard German is used for religious purposes and the Bible is read in High German as are other books and writings of a religious nature.

By the end of eighth grade, children have learned their second language of English and can communicate with non-Amish neighbors. Non-Amish folks are referred to as the English because it is the language used by everybody around them.

...We (the Amish) have our own parochial schools. We have one right there up on the hill and the children come walking, they come from all directions. In Farmerstown they have two. So one gets one end of town and out in the country and the other gets the other end of town and out in the country...

Amish Communities

...There are different orders, you've probably seen different ones and just didn't know it. In the nearby towns of Applecreek and Kidron - and they come all the way down here, you passed one farm. There is one order that is very, very conservative. You really don't want to meet them on a road at night because they hardly have any lights on their buggies. We have to hire someone to take us someplace if we want to go any distance...

...There was this one guy, he had a vanload of people with him and he stopped at a stop sign, and he was just ready to start when here come horses feet right in front of his headlights. And they have one lantern, only one lantern on their buggy and it is on the opposite side. So that horse

had passed and he was just ready to start and here comes another horse. He said I don't know if I'm going to start. He was just so scared. He was from down here and he wasn't used to it but now they can have a lantern on both sides. It's a very, very old order. Their buggies are not marked...

...Around here we have orange signs and lanterns. These old orders say that they don't use the orange signs and lanterns because of their religion. My husband says I don't think it's their religion, I think it's their stubbornness. He said I can't read anything in the Bible where you can't mark your vehicle but maybe he didn't read in the right place I don't know...

Chapter 3:

Quick and Easy Gardening Secrets

... As a child I would get up in time to milk usually 6-6:30. Now I get up at 4:30 and go to bed about 9:30 or 10. It's a long day. There was never a nap time, but now I feel better if I take a very short nap....

The Amish feel a kinship to the earth on many levels. Women design and plant colorful beds of flowers near their houses, barns and vegetable gardens. Farm families do their work according to the rhythm of the seasons using wonderful organizational skills to meet the demands of the crops and stock. Experience builds a farmer's finesse in each area. For instance, making hay requires judging its maturity and dryness as well as storing it properly. These skills are preceded by knowledge of preparing the soil, planting the seeds and controlling the weeds.

The Amish believe that working with soil holds value. They tend a plant, a garden or a farm to stay connected to the earth's growth cycle. They believe that if people are unfamiliar to God's world in nature, they lose who they are.

... I grew up on a farm, so getting up early and milking cows, then breakfast is what we did. Then we would work in the garden. We usually as a family would spade our garden in the fall but that depends on the soil because it will loosen your soil. If you loosen it too early the weeds will start growing. So usually I would wait until spring and now we have tillers so I don't spade it all the time. We would use hand spades and we would put manure in so the whole garden has a layer of manure. That's the fertilizer, and it's still the best fertilizer we can get. Today they use sprays and a tiller. It's different now because we're not on the farm. ...

How do you plant your garden?

Single row planting is placing your seeds in a trench with rows that stretches the length of your garden.

Wide row planting is creating rows up to 3 feet wide and spreading your seeds across the entire area.

Raised-bed planting is building individual mounds of loosely packed soil within rows that stretch the length of your garden. Place your seeds within each mound.

There are many benefits to wide-row planting over single-row planting:

You get more plants per square foot
It's quicker to get your garden in since you don't have to worry about spreading the seeds evenly
The quality of your crops is improved. Since wide-row planting duplicates those conditions naturally found in nature, insect damage is reduced.
Companion planting becomes easier as you can spread more than one type of seed within the row.

Raised-bed planting is recommended if your soil is heavy and doesn't drain properly. Even if you don't have a soil problem, some people just prefer this method. There are less weeds between rows because the ground is more packed from walking between the rows. It is also easier to maintain because you don't have to worry about stepping on plants while watering or harvesting.

...I grew up in Mt Hope. My dad did not spray, he did not use any spray on the weeds when I was growing up. At that time he didn't have to. The weeds would grow in our cornfield. Once every summer we had to go through all our cornfields with a hoe. Dad would cultivate with a horse-drawn cultivator and then we would have to hoe it. So that was a big chore. Once he had gone through it and it was too high for the cultivator, we would go through it. It was usually about my shoulder height. And we would be in there. Now they have no-till. They spray the ground, they don't plow it anymore. They raise the corn no-till. They spray the field and they have these big planters and they plant the corn and they're cultivating nothing. I still think the corn the way dad raised it was a whole lot better than the no-till, and he got a whole lot more. That's a comparison that I think was a whole lot better then, not as many chemicals. By the time they spray to kill the weeds, and they still have to spray the corn and they have

so much chemicals in there, I don't think they have much food value left. I'm not sure what they spray the corn with, but it sure doesn't smell good. I just hate it. When you go by the field and you just know the farmer has just sprayed it, you can smell it. I just get uptight I don't like it. That isn't like the good old days when we did it the hard way...

...Always once we were done we would have a special treat. We would have a hot dog roast and ice cream. That was a very big treat when we were young. The hot dogs were different from what they are now, they were all meat. We also made our own ice cream with strawberries or something on top...

Here are some quick and easy garden tips to help you have a bountiful harvest:

Plant caraway here and there to loosen the soil.

Don't plant fennel in the garden as most plants *Hate* it.

When planting beans, celery or parsley, soak the seeds overnight in water to improve germination.

When planting beets, Swiss chard or peas, soak the seeds about 20 minutes before planting to improve germination.

Avoid overcrowding when planting beets. If you plan to harvest only the tops, plant them 2″ apart. If you plan to harvest the roots, you need 3-4″ between plants.

Sprinkle borox on the ground next to your beet plants to provide boron.

Plant morning glories in your garden to stimulate your melon seeds growth.

If you continue to fertilize your broccoli plants after the first harvest, you will encourage the growth of secondary heads.

Mild frost improves the flavor of brussel sprouts.

Peas are a good plant to have in your garden because they feed the soil.

You will have sweeter tasting tomato plants if you spread baking soda around the plants. It lowers the acidity of the tomatoes as well as keeping away insects.

Plant French marigolds next to tomatoes. The flower deters whiteflies and sagebrush while it stimulates the tomatoes to produce a chemical that repels pests.

The first time you plant your tomato garden, put 1 teaspoon of Epsom® salts in each hole. The salt contains magnesium sulfate which will yield you bigger tomatoes and a larger crop.

Folklore says that a harsh winter is coming if there are thick husks on ears of corn, unusually large crops of acorns or heavy moss growing on the north side of tree trunks.

Poison Ivy

Get rid of poison ivy by mixing 2 gallon soapy water with 3 pounds of salt. Spray this and after a few treatments your problem will be solved.

Grass Stains

For grass stains mix equal parts white vinegar and liquid dishwashing soap into a spray bottle. Spray the area, then let stand awhile before washing. Repeat if necessary before you put the clothes in the dryer as the heat will set the stain.

To get rid of grass stains, try a few drops of full strength vinegar directly on the stain.

Compost

It is best to alternate green matter with brown matter in your compost pile. Greens consist of vegetable and fruit scraps, grass clippings and plant trimmings. Browns consist of newspaper, straw, wood chips and fallen leaves. The green matter will break down a lot faster than the brown.

Control odor in the compost pile with baking soda. Just pour it on – it will help keep the acidity level down.

... I started something last year, it's called the Lasagna Garden. It's layered. You layer your mulch on top of your ground. You can start on grass if you use newspaper or cardboard. It will kill it. I'm surprised because I dug up a toy, I dug up eggshells that were not decayed at all in my leaves. Well you put a layer of garbage on and a layer of peat moss. I didn't put enough peat moss in. So my potatoes did really good and the rest of it I didn't finish until the spring and it should be finished in the fall. So now my tomatoes are just going wild. It's the leaves, the compost and the manure on top. The compost is just the daily garbage. So now for this fall what I'm going to do is put another layer of compost on it, peat moss, leaves and manure. I learned that when I put eggshells on it I have to crush it, really crush it so they will break up. Also slugs cannot live in eggshells so I thought well good enough, those can stay in there for years and years. I don't really care. When the slugs hit them it cuts through that protection they have, that slimy protection. ...

Herbs

Decorate your herb garden with treasures from flea markets and garage sales. Some ideas are old wooden wheelbarrows, garden gates, wagon wheels, old water pumps or whirligigs.

If you want to grow lavender, be sure you have plenty of lime in the soil.

Herbs love lime and soil that is gritty. Provide this by adding one handful of ground oyster shells into the hole before you plant the herbs.

Herbs in the Kitchen

A good way to store fresh herbs is to use salt. Cover the bottom of a glass container with a layer of uniodized or kosher salt. Add one layer of herbs. Repeat ending with a layer of salt. Seal with an airtight lid, and store in a cool, dry place. To use the herbs, just rinse them off.

Garlic oil or any herb oil is great for cooking but you must make it properly. Several botulism deaths were traced to garlic stored in oil. Here are some safety tips:

Add either vinegar or lemon juice to your herbal oil. Use 1 tablespoon per cup of oil.

Always keep herbal oils refrigerated. Use all herbal oils within one week.

Another way to preserve herbs for cooking is by making herbal butter. Good combinations are basil, rosemary, sage, thyme and marjoram. Take one stick of unsalted butter at room temperature and add 3 teaspoons of fresh, minced herbs and 1/2 teaspoon of lemon juice. Combine with a fork. Store in the refrigerator and use within 3 days. You can also freeze it for use within 3 months.

...In some ways, it is lots stricter now then it was, and in other ways not, as far as material things. It doesn't matter what time we have. There's things the English farmers have, things that are a lot more modern than they did when I was a girl. So it's easier for the farmer to do his work, but he doesn't have nearly as much money left over as before. At that time when my dad was doing the farming, that's when they could make money. Now they can't. The feed is too expensive...

Children & Gardening

Pique your child's interest in gardening from an early age. Help them write their name in the soil with a stick. Then plant seeds so they can see their name in flowers.

In the pumpkin patch, write a child's name on the young pumpkin as soon as it is big enough to write on. Apply enough pressure to bruise the skin and watch the name grow along with the pumpkin.

Moss

Prevent moss from growing by sprinkling baking soda around the area.

Lawn

Mix flour with your fertilizer to avoid over fertilizing and burning your lawn. The flour makes it easy to see where you have fertilized. One rainfall will wash it away.

Garden Hose

Has your garden hose sprung a leak? Poke more holes the whole length of the hose. It makes a great misting soaker for the garden.

Create a tree brace with an old garden hose. Cut it in sections long enough to wrap around the tree. When a young tree needs support, slip your rope or wire through the hose and around the tree to the stake in the ground. The hose protects the bark from being gouged from the wire.

Use your garden hose to visualize the basic design of your shrub beds.

Germ Free

Be sure to scrub the skin of fruits and melons with water and a brush. This must be done before cutting the fruit to prevent the transfer of pathogens from the rind to the flesh.

Garden Chores

Wear an oven mitt when pruning your rose bush to protect against the thorns.

When doing garden chores like raking, digging and hoeing, alternate your grip to avoid injury from the repetitive motion.

Put a fabric softener sheet around your neck while gardening to ward off pests.

Garden Problem Solvers

Protect your lettuce and cabbage from being eaten before you can get to them. Just cover your plants with a mesh potato bag.

Keep your fingernails clean while gardening by scraping soap under your nails before beginning. This makes for easy cleanup.

Houseplants

Plant containers don't just have to be pots. They can be almost anything, just be sure you add some drainage holes in the bottom. Try using grandpa's old work boots, grandma's old watering can, baskets, tin cups, mom's teapot, old tins, pottery, seashells, etc.

Repair the stem of houseplants by making a splint with toothpicks and soft tape. The plant often will mend itself.

Another way to repair houseplant stems is with transparent tape alone. Again, the plant often will mend itself.

Feed your houseplants with club soda that has lost its fizz.

If you have a water softener, be sure you don't use water from the tap to water your houseplants. The sodium makes the soil sticky and is toxic to some plants. Use bottled water or rainwater. If you absolutely must use water from the tap that is connected to a water softener, add 1/2 teaspoon of calcium sulfate (gypsum) per gallon of softened water before you water your plants.

Talk to your plants – they love the carbon dioxide you exhale!

To refresh an ailing fern, mix 1 tablespoon castor oil and 1 tablespoon baby shampoo to 2 pints of warm water. Feed the plant wit 3 tablespoons of the solution.

Ferns do well indoors if you avoid direct sunlight. Add extra peat to the soil. Ferns are sensitive to chemical insecticides and air or water pollution – so don't water from your tap if you have a water softener.

Spider plants do not like drafts. Keep the soil moist in spring and summer and drier in fall and winter.

Clean Flowers, Clean Tools

Clean clay flower pots with baking soda and water.

To clean plants, use 1/2 cup baking soda per 1 gallon of cold water. This works for real plants as well as silk ones.

If you're one of those that "plant" silk flowers in hanging baskets or worse yet silk azalea bushes, here's how to clean them: Put the flowers into a pillowcase and tie it shut. Place it into your dryer along with a wet washcloth for 20 minutes. Use the no heat setting to fluff.

Clean your lawn mower blades by applying cooking spray to the clean blades before mowing. It makes cleaning the grass off the blades much easier. You can also use the spray to clean the entire mower. Just spray and wipe.

Rust Fighters

Before putting your garden tools away for the winter, spray them with penetrating oil to prevent rust.

Another way to protect your tools from rust is to coat them with petroleum jelly.

Trees

Be sure to prune away dead limbs and vegetation from trees and shrubs.

Prune the sprouts that grow at the base of your trees.

When mulching your trees, be sure the mulch is at least 5 inches away from the trunk of the tree on all sides.

Flowers

Always fertilize your rose bushes monthly. Be sure to water thoroughly the day before your fertilize.

A good fertilizer for outside flowers is a solution of 4 parts cola to 1 part water. Use every month.

Plant violets at the bottom of hedges as that is where they grow naturally.

Perk up your cut flowers!...Add some 7-UP® to the vase.

...or put 2 tablespoons each of sugar and white vinegar to one quart of warm water. The sugar provides food for the flowers and the vinegar helps prevent bacteria.

...or give the flowers an aspirin – just add it to the vase.

Add some boric acid to the vase to keep carnations fresh longer.

Add a teaspoon of sugar to the vase to prevent marigolds from leaving an odor.

Sugar water added to the vase will keep chrysanthemums fresh longer.

Put a copper penny in the vase with tulips to keep them from opening up too wide.

Rosebuds will open quicker with a teaspoon of sugar added to the vase.

When flower stems are too short, try using a straw. Just place the stem in a clear drinking straw and add it to the vase.

Place a coffee filter on the very bottom of flower pots to prevent the dirt from coming out of the drainage holes.

Use the net bags that your onions come in on the bottom of your flower pots as drainage for the soil.

Don't plant strong scented flowers like lily-of-the-valley if you or a family members suffers from asthma as the scent can bring on an asthma attack.

Put daffodils in a vase of their own because they have a negative effect on other flowers.

Never water your outside flowers at night. Wet leaves left overnight make the plant more susceptible to fungal disease. The best time for watering is early in the morning. Be sure you water clear down to the roots.

For the best African violet plants, push some rusty nails into the soil near the plant.

African violets do very well under fluorescent lights. Do not cut off damaged leaves, pull them off instead.

Give your azaleas a boost with 2 tablespoons of white vinegar into 1 quart of water.

Hollow out an old stump to make an unusual flower pot for your landscape. Just fill it with good soil and go!

The scarlet pimpernel is also known as the *poor man's weatherglass*. When the flowers close during the day it is a sign of rain.

Planting Secrets

Mark the rows in your garden by simply inserting a wooden pencil in the ground. Place the seed packet over the pencil to identify where the seeds are planted.

If your soil is alkaline, just cover the ground with a milk vinegar solution

Azaleas love acetic soil and vinegar is a good fertilizer for them. Make a solution with a 1/2 cup apple cider vinegar to 1 gallon of water. Water the plants with this solution once a month.

Radishes also like acetic soil, use the same mixture as you did for the azaleas.

Neutralize soil that is too acidic by covering the ground with baking soda.

If you change the pH levels of your garden from acid to alkaline or vice versa, be careful what you plant in that location next season. Don't try to plant an acid loving plant in alkaline soil.

To warm up the soil, cover the ground with clear plastic until it is time to plant. It lets in more heat than black plastic does.

Make sure that you rotate the location of your tomato garden each year because the tomatoes rob the soil of magnesium.

When planting tiny seeds, it is helpful to mix them with dry sand. It helps to distribute the seeds more evenly. Dry sand can be purchased at your local hardware store or nurseries.

Growing Hints

Strengthen young plants with straws. Just cut the straw to the proper length and wrap it around the stem of the plant for support.

Start plant seedlings in a wax-free paper cup filled with potting soil. When it's time for the plant to continue growing outside, just place the cup right into the garden. The cup is biodegradable.

Support small plants with a paper cup. Simply cut an "X" on the bottom, turn the cup upside down and place over the plant for support.

If you love cantaloupe but have a small garden, panty hose can help! Use a trellis for the plant to grow on and let the hose hold the melons as they grow. An old bra works just as well but you may not like its appearance as well!

Place growing melons on the top of an upside down coffee can. It keeps insects and other pests away and will generate heat to help ripen the fruit sooner.

Start your tomato plants with a 2 liter plastic cola bottle. Cut off the top and use the bottom as a pot to start the plants.

Change locations for your garden vegetables each year to reduce disease and pests. It also helps to restore the nutrients in the soil.

Try hanging black plastic behind your eggplant garden to reflect the heat.

To improve the flavor of endive before you harvest it, loosely tie the outer leaves with string for two weeks.

Plant garlic cloves 2″ deep and 5″ apart. Make sure you water generously during hot weather. When the foliage begins to shrivel at the end of summer, it is time to harvest the bulbs. Tie them in bunches and dry in the sun.

Lettuce, Swiss chard, spinach and parsley grows best away from intense sunlight and in a partially shaded spot.

For faster growing tomatoes, peppers and eggplants, add magnesium by mixing 2 tablespoons Epsom® salts to 1 gallon water. When the plant begins to bloom, apply one pint of the mixture to each plant.

Use old pantyhose to tie up tomatoes, melons, squash and cucumbers.

Fertilizer

An effective and inexpensive fertilizer can be made by mixing 1 capful of ammonia with one gallon of water. Be sure not to increase this ratio.

Add one half can of regular cola per one gallon of water and use to revive your plants.

Give your plants a nitrogen boost by dissolving one packet of unflavored gelatin into one quart of water. Use this mixture once a month.

... I do a lot of Epsom® salts. I use a lot of Epsom® salts. It is like a fertilizer. You don't see any slugs if you have Epsom® salts around your plants because that too will cut through that slime. I planted some Hibiscus along the road and two weeks ago they were just a gob of color. The ones up here were a little bit smaller and I thought why? The others get all the salt off the road, so I threw Epsom® salts on these. So I think that's the secret, they want Epsom® salts. But that's the only thing I give my hibiscus. There's one up here, a young one I just started last year and it had huge blooms and I put some Epsom® salts on them and I could see the difference. I use it too on lettuce and my strawberry plants...

Pests

Are the ants loving your cantaloupe? Spray the perimeter of the plant with vinegar and the ants will stay away. Just be careful not to use too much vinegar that you change the pH level of the soil.

A quick way to tell if a bug you spot in your garden is friend or foe...If it moves fast, it's a friend, slow means foe.

Make your own natural pesticide with 1 tablespoon white vinegar, 1 tablespoon liquid dish soap and 1/2 gallon of water. Spray directly onto your plants to get rid of insects.

Repel bugs from zucchini and pumpkin plants with this hint: Poke a few holes in aluminum foil and place it under your plants. The reflection will keep away damaging bugs, reflect the sunlight, and still allow water to penetrate the soil.

A couple of tablespoons of beer and water makes a good pesticide when sprayed on your houseplants.

Instead of using pesticide on cabbage, brussels sprouts, broccoli and cauliflower, just sprinkle the heads with baking soda to keeps pests away. Reapply it after it rains.

To keep beetles away from your garden, sprinkle your plants with a mixture of baking soda and cayenne pepper.

Sprinkle coffee grounds around carrot plants to repel root maggots.

... Epsom® salts also kill slugs. I don't see slugs on plants as the salt cuts thru their slimy skin. Actually a friend told me about this and I came home and tried it. I dissolved about a cup of Epsom® salts in a two gallon watering can and sprinkled my peas and my strawberries. Later on my daughter said, hey you don't have all those bugs chomping in my face when I pick strawberries. I didn't really realize that it took care of the bugs. I go with that a lot...

Weeds

May is the critical time of the season to control weeds in your garden. Mulching deprives the weeds of sunlight, and be sure to replenish the mulch after weeding. A garden that is well-mulched will only need to be weeded two to three times during the season.

Pour salt in your gravel driveway to kill grass and weeds.

Control weeds in your flower bed by laying down a layer of black plastic. Poke holes in the plastic to plant your flowers and add mulch. The holes allow water to penetrate the soil and will cut down on weeds.

Weeds and grass growing in the cracks of your sidewalk or patio?...pour full strength vinegar or boiling salt water onto the weeds.

...or spread salt or baking soda into the cracks to prevent the weeds and grass from growing.

Doing your weeding after a heavy rain makes the job a lot easier.

Weeding – it's the job we all hate. Although I do have a few friends who swear that weeding is a great stress-reducer! Regardless of whether you like it or not, it must be done – and done routinely. If not, the weeds will leech all the water and nutrients out of the soil, attract insects and the result will be unhealthy plants and a limited harvest.

Make sure that you work the soil immediately before planting. When you rake, you are stirring up hundreds of weed seedlings that die off when disturbed. If you let the ground sit a few days and then plant, the weeds have a chance to germinate again. So plant your seeds right after you rake the prepared ground.

Once you plant your garden, you must keep after the weeds – even after you've harvested your crop.

...Farmers have more modern conveniences than when I was a girl. The Amish are always a hop behind. There's not nearly as much money left over as before. Feed has gotten too expensive. You can't make any money. When I was a girl we would feed the chickens and sell the eggs and that would be our grocery money. Now you have to pay out of your pocket

for the feed. We would get the mash from the grain elevator in town. And Oyster Shells. Dad would always see to it that we mixed some in, some crushed oyster shells. We just had a pan sitting in there on the chicken coop. By eating some of that, the eggs would get harder. By the chickens eating that, the oyster shells, the eggs would be harder so they would not break so easily. Now there is no way you can do it. The feed is too expensive and the eggs pretty much stayed the same price...

Watering

Poke holes in the bottom of 1 gallon plastic milk jugs and bury them next to your plants. When it rains the jugs will fill with water and provide a continuous watering for the plant.

Plants need water the most right after they blossom and the fruit is starting to form. Make sure the soil is loose before you water your garden so the water is absorbed. Water slowly to a depth of about 6 inches. You want to be careful not to overwater your garden as that can cause the roots to rot. If you're not sure, you can buy a moisture meter to tell you when you need to water.

Soil

Your soil has to be healthy for your plants to grow nicely as plants get their nutrients from the minerals in the soil. The texture is also important. The best garden soil contains approximately 45% sand, 35% silt and 20% clay with the balance being made up of organic matter.

The pH level of the soil will determine how well your plants can use the nutrients that are present. You need to know the pH levels in your soil, so head to your local garden center and get a soil test kit.

If the pH level is above 7, that means your soil is alkaline and you need to add acid. *The fix?* Add horse or chicken manure or sulphur.

If the pH level is below 7, that means your soil is acid. You do need a certain amount of acidity for your plants to do well. But if it is below 6, you need to raise the alkaline. *The fix?* Add ground limestone or oyster shells.

A Word About Earthworms...

As disgusting as it may sound, the castings of earthworms are abundant with components that all plants need such as nitrates, calcium, phosphates and potash. They also contain other trace elements that help keep plants healthy. Use them in your garden for better tasting plants and larger harvests.

Castings will not hurt any plant and will even help to revive sick or dying plants. Simply replace some of the potting soil with the castings.

Pot your plants with a mixture of 2/3 peat moss or soil and 1/3 castings. Be sure to water thoroughly.

When planting your garden, seeds will germinate quicker when castings are used. It will also help to produce hardy rosebushes.

I'm sure you are thinking, "How am I supposed to get a hold of earthworm castings?" The answer is simple. They are available in packages at your local garden supply store.

Let's talk about grass...

In the United States over $25 billion is spent on over 67 million pounds of pesticides each year. Where is it used? On lawns.

Does your front lawn stick out in your neighborhood like a sore thumb? You know what I mean, all brown and burnt out by the middle of summer? Well, it doesn't have to be that way anymore.

Everybody wants their lawn to be lush and green. But how does it get that way? The best tip I can give you is to mow properly. According to Trey Rogers, an associate professor of Turf Grass Science at Michigan State University, "Seventy percent of the problems we have with lawns are directly or indirectly related to the way homeowners mow."

His 3 rules when it comes to mowing:

1. Never cut your grass more than one-third its height during any one mowing. This will give the lawn a chance

to feed properly and grow more densely, leaving weeds with no place to grow.
2. Alternate mowing patterns. East to west, then north to south, then diagonal mowing will prevent the stress of ruts and compacting of the soil caused by repeated mowing in the same direction.
3. Leave grass clippings on the lawn. They provide important nutrients for the soil and is not the source problem for thatch.

It is better to water the lawn less often but do the job right. Soak the soil to at least a depth of six inches. Light sprinkles more often will just weaken the roots and make them vulnerable to disease.

Never water the grass at night as that makes it more susceptible to fungal disease. The best time of day to water your lawn is in the early morning.

If you've been reaaaaally busy with no time to mow and suddenly your grass is knee high – well maybe not that bad – but high, here's what to do: It is less stressful for the grass to mow a couple of inches at a time at different times than to mow it all at once. By mowing in stages you'll have less grass clippings at one time – which by the way are good for the soil. The overall height of your grass should be about 3 inches all the time. Any shorter and you run the risk of it burning out, plus the higher grass will prevent the weeds and crabgrass from getting sunlight.

Ground Cover

If you are looking for ground cover around trees or any shady spot, your best bet is pachysandra. Other choices are bugle weed, campanula or periwinkle.

If you need ground cover for a sunny area, try bear berry, creeping thyme, honeysuckle, sedum or star jasmine.

Wildflowers can add special interest to your garden. Some of the varieties needing sun are blazing star, giant evening primrose, elephantheads, butterfly weed, golden stars, scarlet sage, cosmos, purple cone flower, and Our Lord's candle. Some of the types that need shade are wild ginger, purple trillium, white trillium, white baneberry and shinleaf.

Chapter 4:

Food Remedies for your Garden

One in three Amish breadwinners makes their living from agriculture. The youngest child inherits the farm. Tourists assume the oldest child inherits, but the practice is a pattern of inheritance practiced in many of the German-speaking areas of Europe. It allows the Amish father to be useful with employment for a longer time before he retires. The child is expected to provide a place for the parents to live called the grandparent or "dawdy haus" and it is attached to or next to the main house. The income that the parents receive from the sale of the farm is used in their retirement. They still help with the farm and the grandchildren though. They also grow their own garden.

Amish families face a daily work agenda that is foreign to an American household where most needs are supplied through stores or mail order houses. For the Amish, clothing and feeding a family includes sewing their traditional garb and growing foods to preserve. Many keep the house and garden clean and trimmed to a standard close to perfection. In an Amish household, there is work to do all day every day. A family working together lives out a work ethic that has been the backbone of Amish traditions. It implies that even the youngest can help. Sharing responsibilities like picking vegetables and milking twice a day draws a family together.

Food and scraps from your table can be a friend to your garden. Sometimes one food helps another to grow. Other times there is a food that helps another once it is harvested. There are many common foods from your garden that will assist you in many ways like keeping bugs out of your pantry, reducing salty tasting foods, preventing fruit from turning brown and helping flowers to grow. There's cleaning and storing tips, freezing and crisping hints and lots and lots in between! That's what this chapter is about – your food – and what it can do for you.

Keep Food Fresh

Keep cut apples from turning brown by spraying them with lemon juice. Orange or grapefruit juice works too.

Store asparagus by standing them in about 1 inch of cold water and cover with a plastic bag.

If your asparagus has gone limp, simply cut off the ends and stand them in some cold water. Cover with a plastic bag and refrigerate.

Make celery crisp again by putting it a bowl of ice water along with some raw potato slices. They should be good and crunchy in an hour.

Put the crisp back in veggies, fill the bin of your refrigerator with brown paper bags to keep your garden produce crisp.

Line the vegetable bin of your refrigerator with brown paper bags to keep your garden produce crisp.

Keep cucumbers in the vegetable bin in your refrigerator. They get mushy when they get too cold.

To revive wilted parsley, cut a little of the stem and stand in a glass of ice water. Refrigerate 1 hour.

Onions will last longer if they are stored where the air can circulate around them. A clean, old pair of pantyhose will do the trick. Just keep them in a leg and tie it up.

Odor

To reduce the smell of cooking cabbage, drop a whole walnut – including the shell - into the pan.

Another way of reducing the smell of cabbage when cooking is to add a stalk of celery to the pot.

If you left some garden produce or other food in the refrigerator too long and now you have an odor problem, here's what to do: Crumple up brown paper bags and put one on each shelf of the refrigerator. Keep replacing them until the smell is gone.

Another way to get rid of food odor is with coffee grounds. Put a small bowl on each shelf of the refrigerator until the odor is gone.

Helpful Food Hints

Do you love beans but hate the gas? Try this: Tie up some fennel seeds in a cloth to make a little bag. Soak it overnight in water with your beans. Then remove the seeds and add fresh water and a quartered potato. Remove the potato pieces when the beans are done.

One thing I hate about celery is the strings. Peel the celery stalk with a potato peeler and say begone to the strings!

Remove the silk from ears of corn with a damp paper towel.

When re-heating leftover meat, put clean lettuce leaves on aluminum foil. Put the meat on top of leaves and seal the foil. The lettuce will add moisture to the meat as it heats.

After harvesting and cleaning peas in their pods, cook in boiling water. When the pods rise to the top, the peas are done and ready to be shelled.

Added too much salt during cooking? Just take a raw, peeled potato and cut it up. Add it to the pot and it will absorb the excess salt.

To remove excess fat from soups or stews, simply do this. Remove the pan from heat and lay a couple of lettuce leafs on the top. In a few minutes the leaves will have absorbed the grease.

When cooking a roast, try adding a couple of ounces of strong tea. It will tenderize the meat as well as reduce cooking time.

> *Pliny the Elder,* a Roman scholar and natu-
> ralist, said that to prevent nightmares one
> should eat cabbage before going to sleep.

If you have a crop of yellow onions and hate the strong taste, try this: Cut them in thin slices and place them in a pan. Pour boiling water over the onions and add some white vinegar. Let them be for a couple of minutes. Drain, cover & refrigerate. When the onions are cold, they will taste like sweet onions.

To soften brown sugar, add a few slices of apple to the container and keep the lid tightly closed. A couple of days should do the trick. Lemons and oranges work well for this too.

Sweeten tomato sauce by adding some grated carrots. It sweetens naturally without sugar.

To ripen green tomatoes, put them in a bag with some apples and store in a cool, dark area. The ethylene gas that the apples emit help the tomatoes ripen quicker.

Cut off the leafy tops of root vegetables before you store them so all of the nutrients stay in the vegetable.

After your spaghetti dinner, save the water from cooking the pasta. Let it cool, then use it to water your plants. The starch in the water is good for them.

Fun Garnishes

Freeze grapes for use in salads, garnishes, punch or even as a snack.

Freeze fresh herbs in ice cube trays. When the recipe calls for it, just drop in a cube.

While you're at it, put lemon twists in the ice cubes for lemonade or whole cherries, orange twists, a sprig of mint or edible flowers in other beverages.

Cooking with Herbs

If a recipe calls for fresh herbs you can substitute dried herbs. You must use 3 times the amount of dried herb than you would if using fresh.

When adding fresh herbs, crumble them in your hand a little to release more of the flavor.

Preserve fresh ginger root in sherry. Seal in a glass jar and store in your refrigerator. The longer it is in there, the sherry develops a ginger taste, but the ginger will never taste like sherry.

Store ginger root with potatoes to make both the potatoes and the ginger last longer.

Don't use metal teapots to make herbal tea. The metal affects the chemistry of the tea.

Allergies

Anyone with an allergy to ragweed or grass pollen may get an itchy mouth or throat after eating cantaloupe.

Anyone with an allergy to birch pollen may get an itchy mouth after eating carrots.

Anyone with asthma may be extremely allergic to dried potatoes, hash browns or french fries treated with sulfates.

Spinach should be avoided by anyone who suffers from gout because of the purines it contains.

Strawberries and tomatoes should be avoided by anyone allergic to aspirin

Anyone allergic to ragweed, tomatoes, and grass pollen should avoid eating watermelon.

For Plants

Tear banana peels into small pieces and bury them around your rose bushes to provide phosphorus and potash.

Protect your chrysanthemums, azaleas and roses with this spray: Grind together 3 hot peppers, 1 large garlic bulb and 4 large onions. Cover with water overnight. Then strain it and add enough water to make 1 gallon.

Water your plants with the water left from hard-boiling eggs, steaming vegetables or even use the old water left from cleaning the aquarium.

For Flowers

Help your cut flowers last longer with a mixture of 2 tablespoons vinegar and 2 tablespoons maple syrup added to the vase of water. If you prefer, you can use 1 tablespoon sugar in place of the maple syrup.

Bugs

Mix orange juice and orange peels in a food processor and blend. Pour it down ant hills to get rid of ants.

To prevent creepy crawlers in your pantry try putting a few bay leaves or whole cloves on the shelves. Black pepper or cayenne pepper will also work, but it's a little messy.

Place cucumber or pieces of mint gum on your kitchen shelves to deter ants.

To kill any insects hiding in your lettuce, cabbage, broccoli and cauliflower, just soak the vegetables in the sink with water and vinegar.

Compost

Crush your eggshells and use these as compost. Walnut shells and fish scraps work good too.

Banana peels, orange rinds, lemon rinds, apple peels, melon rinds, vegetable peels and potato skins all make good compost material.

Save your coffee grounds, and ask your friend to save theirs for you too. It makes great compost. You can use the filter and all.

...Table scraps make the best compost for an organic garden. Potato skins work the best but anything from the table is good. Just keep adding to it. Of course I layer it with peat moss, leaves and manure...

You can add nutrients to the soil by adding organic matter. The best way to do this is by composting. It is easy to do, and if you ask ten gardeners for the best way to compost, you'll get ten answers! Here are several to get you started:

Make sure your compost pile is at least three feet wide in all directions. This will insure that enough heat is created to create compost. Spread your compost material along with a layer of dirt and water it down. Every so often turn the pile over working from the center on out. This provides oxygen that assists in breaking down the organic matter.

Be sure to cover your compost pile during a rainstorm so the best stuff doesn't wash away.

Crush your eggshells and use these as compost.

Use all your grass clippings, weeds, hedge clippings and leaves in your compost pile. You should have plenty of material by using this source. Just be sure to spread it thin.

Sprinkle light layers of wood ashes. Walnut shells work good too.

Fish scraps make good compost if you bury it in the middle of the compost pile.

If you have a bird, every time you clean the cage throw the whole mess in your compost pile.

Newspaper works well. You can also use paper from your paper shredder. Cover it with some hay to keep it in place.

Don't put meat or bones in your compost pile because it attracts rats.

The best activator for a compost pile is alfalfa meal. You can find it at any feed store.

Don't throw diseased plants into your compost pile!

How can you tell if your compost pile is doing its job? It should smell sweet and earthy and look dark and crumbly. If it stinks, you may have over watered it. Add some wood chips or leaves to soak up the water. Be sure you are tossing the pile regularly from the outside of the pile into the center.

...I also go with the Organic Gardening. I go with the more natural things. All natural, partly the compost, partly the manure. I have my garden in two parts because I like to use my seeder and plant my corn without the manure. I don't know maybe I'll try it sometime, but I don't think I'd ever have enough manure to cover the whole big garden. I don't use pesticides. Well I can't say that. I have Eggplant but eggplant

it is so hard to grow. It has so many bugs on it. I finally gave up and sprayed that with the pesticide and it started to bloom and grow. I wish it was as easy to grow as zucchini you can just plant those and forget it...

Clean Produce

Clean your produce with Jay Kordich, The Juiceman's method: Fill the sink with cold water and add 4 tablespoons salt and the juice from half a lemon. Though diluted, this is actually a form of hydrochloric acid. Soak fruits and vegetables for 10 minutes, berries for 3 minutes.

For Your Picnic

When heading out to the picnic, wrap the watermelon in newspaper and transport it that way. The newspaper will keep the melon cool and fresh.

Planting Hints

Cabbage, broccoli and cauliflower plants need extra calcium. Provide this by mixing crushed egg shells into the soil around the plants.

To prevent worms in your onion plants, layer used coffee grounds that have been dried in the bottom of the row before you plant.

To prevent club root, boil rhubarb leaves in boiling water and sprinkle on the soil before seeds.

To protect flowers and plants from blight, make an infusion of elderberry leaves in warm water and sprinkle it over the plants.

Some Beauty Hints...

Acne

For acne, make a lemon balm infusion and apply directly to the area. Apply it each evening at bedtime.

For skin blemishes, combine 1 ripe banana with 2 tablespoons of chamomile tea. Use a cotton ball to dab the mixture onto blemishes to form a mask. After 5 minutes, rinse off with cool water.

Brown Spots

To remove brown spots on the face and hands, grind fresh parsley and use the juice directly onto the spots. Apply it each evening at bedtime.

Dandruff

Make this Herbal Antiseptic Vinegar for dandruff: Coarsely chop 1/2 cup fresh or dried oregano and 1/2 cup fresh or dried lavender buds. Place in wide mouth canning jar. Add 2 cups apple cider vinegar, being sure to completely cover the herbs. Gently push the herbs down into the vinegar, stirring to release air bubbles. Cover with a lid and store for two weeks at room temperature. Be sure to keep it away from direct sunlight. *If using a metal lid, first cover the jar with wax paper to prevent corrosion.*

For dandruff: Shampoo and rinse hair as usual. Then use 2 tablespoons of the vinegar per 1 cup warm water and massage into scalp. Do not re-rinse.

Stings

Soothe a wasp sting with a drop of basil oil.

Wrinkles

A lemon balm infusion will soften wrinkles. Apply to the skin each morning.

Chapter 5:

Amish Gardening

The silhouette of a horse and buggy is the most frequently used illustration on billboards, signs and tourist ads to promote tourism. It is a significant outer symbol of Amish religious values and distinctive lifestyle. Standardbred horses pull the buggies used for transportation. These are bought from racehorse owners that are not good enough for racing or have become too old. Draft horses are used on the farm for plowing, disking, planting, harvesting and other field work. They are usually Belgians or Percherons, relatives to the Clydesdale.

Children learn responsibility be tending often 200 chickens and two cows. They make and peddle butter, eggs and produce along a regular route. They often get up as early as 5AM even on school days. The father feels that this routine helps them face the realities of responsibility that is always there. Children understand the importance of hoeing and mulching to reduce weeding. They learn at a young age that crops must be harvested when they're ready, that everything has its season. Give children the privilege of caring for plants until they produce a flower or food to eat. Observe how tending the earth and the passing of time work together during the growing season.

... I helped my brothers with his chores sometimes. The boys helped with farm chores, feed the animals, bed them down, get straw down from the loft. That was a job because straw wasn't baled at that time. You had to do it with a pitch fork. It was a lot of work. I just can't remember that I helped very often with that. I would go feed the chickens and then take care of the eggs and that was my duty. When it was cold in the winter my dad would do it because he didn't have so much to do. I would help mom. Another thing was to get the wood and coal in from the wood shed, fill all the wood boxes, see that the all the lanterns, gas lights and oil lamps were all filled because in the winter it took a lot of it....

Herbal Remedies for your Garden

Scatter caraway plants in your garden to loosen the soil.

Keep fennel plants away from your garden as most plants hate it.

Plant yarrow near aromatic herbs because it will enhance the production of essential oils. It is a good border plant.

Protect your roses and raspberry plants by planting garlic nearby.

Chives are a good companion to roses.

Garlic likes roses and peach trees.

Parsley enhances the scent of roses & protects them from insects.

Comfrey is known as a plant doctor because it keeps the soil moist and rich. It is high in Vitamin C and A, and its deep roots don't rob minerals from the soil's surface from other plants nearby.

Companion Planting

Since the old days, gardeners know that some plants just seem to thrive when planted nearby certain other plants.

Asparagus *Love* tomatoes, nasturtiums, parsley and basil. They *Hate* onions, garlic and gladiolus.

Basil *Loves* tomatoes, green peppers and asparagus. *Hates* rue.

Beans *Love* potatoes, carrots, peas, cauliflower, eggplant, cucumbers, corn, rosemary and petunias. They *Hate* onions and garlic.

Beets *Love* cabbage, lettuce and onions. They *Hate* pole beans.

Broccoli, Cauliflower and Cabbage *Love* carrots, beets, lettuce, spinach, onions, cucumbers, potatoes, celery, dill, sage, rosemary, thyme, chamomile, hyssop and nasturtiums. They *Hate* strawberries and tomatoes.

Cantaloupes *Love* corn and they don't hate anybody!

Carrots Love beans, peas, tomatoes, onions, peppers, cabbage, chives, rosemary and sage. They **Hate** dill, celery and parsnips.

Corn Loves beans, peas, cucumbers, cantaloupes, squash, cabbage, parsley and pumpkin and they don't hate anybody!

Cucumbers Love beans, peas, corn, tomatoes, cabbage, lettuce, radishes, sunflowers, chamomile, dill and nasturtiums. They **Hate** potatoes and sage.

Dill Loves cabbage and **Hates** carrots.

Eggplant Loves beans, garlic and peppers and they don't hate anybody!

Lettuce Loves beets, carrots, strawberries, cabbage, onions, basil and cucumbers and they don't hate anybody!

Garlic and Onions Love beets, tomatoes, broccoli, peppers, lettuce, cabbage, carrots, strawberries, chamomile, parsnips and turnips. They **Hate** beans, peas and asparagus.

Hyssop Loves grapes and cabbage and **Hates** radishes.

Parsley Loves asparagus, tomatoes and corn and they don't hate anybody!

Peas Love radishes, carrots, cucumbers, corn, beans, turnips, and potatoes. They **Hate** onions, garlic and gladiolus.

Potatoes Love beans, cabbage, corn, peas, marigolds, eggplant, parsnips, dead nettle and horseradish (if planted at the corner of the plot). They **Hate** pumpkin, squash, cucumbers, turnips, tomatoes, sunflowers and raspberries.

Pumpkins Love corn, eggplant and radishes. They **Hate** potatoes.

Radishes Love peas, nasturtiums, cucumbers, carrots and parsnips. They **Hate** hyssop.

Rue Loves rosemary and roses and **Hates** sweet basil.

Sage _Loves_ Rosemary and _Hates_ cucumbers.

Spinach _Loves_ cabbage and strawberries and they don't hate anybody!

Squash _Love_ corn, borage and nasturtiums. They _Hate_ potatoes.

Strawberries _Love_ spinach, beans, onions, borage and lettuce (if planted as a border). They _Hate_ cabbage.

Tomatoes _Love_ asparagus, peppers, celery, onions, carrots, cucumbers, basil, parsley, chives, borage, marigolds and nasturtiums. They _Hate_ dill, potatoes and cabbage.

For centuries, herbs have been used medicinally to treat illness. They play an important role in Chinese medicine and in the Indian ayurvedic system. They are widely accepted as medicinal treatment in Europe. The early settlers in this country brought herbs with them for healing uses. During the 19th century, herbs began to be used to beautify the home, a practice that continues today.

There are many foods and herbs that we grow in our gardens that can provide healing remedies and first aid to our bodies. What follows is an assortment of these uses and tonics.

Aloe

Pure aloe is very effective for minor burns, wounds and skin irritations. The immediate application of sap from the leaf will reduce the pain and speed the healing process.

Apples

Apples are a great source of fiber. Adding this to your diet can help prevent colon cancer and improve cholesterol. The high fiber they contain will fill you up with fewer calories.

Foods sweetened with fructose (fruit, soda & juice – especially apple & pear juice) and sorbitol (sugarless gum & candy) may produce intestinal gas. Spread your intake over the entire day so your system isn't hit all at once.

One eight-ounce glass of apple juice has 295 mg. of potassium. This is more than contained in half a banana, plus it contains boron which helps maintain healthy bones. *Note:* Daily consumption of apple or grapefruit juice can increase the risk of kidney stones.

Are you an apple? Apple shaped women carry more fat around the middle and have a greater risk of heart disease.

Basil

Basil means different things in different cultures. The ancient Romans and Greeks used it in purification rites and exorcism. In 16th century Europe, lovers would exchange basil as a sign of faithfulness. In Mexico, many would carry basil in their pocket to attract money and good luck.

Basil's folklore is even practiced in modern times. Some will carry a piece of basil along when traveling to insure a safe return home. Others wear the oil or carry a basil sachet when involved in competitions or contests. Shop owners in Europe sprinkle it around their stores for protection and to promote prosperity.

There are many different kinds of basil, but the most common is Sweet basil. It is commonly used in cooking to enhance the flavor of food. It also has many medicinal uses.

It can be used to help a cough by combining the juice with equal parts honey. It is also a good remedy for bad breath.

Try a cup of basil tea for indigestion and stomach cramps. Since it also has some sedative properties, it will also help nervous headaches and anxiety.

Using too much salt? Cut back by using more basil!

Apply one drop of basil oil on your pillow at night to help insomnia and depression.

Basil should not be taken medicinally by pregnant women.

Since basil is an annual, you will have to plant it every year. Basil leaves can be dried and stored in glass jars or plastic bags – but be sure to store them in a dark place. You can also freeze basil leaves: Dab both sides of the leave thoroughly with olive oil and store in a freezer bag. In either case, be sure the leaves are clean.

You can also store basil in oil by grinding the leaves in a food processor and adding enough olive oil to make a paste. Store in the refrigerator for up to two months.

Beans

Beans are loaded with protein, fiber, vitamins & minerals – and are low in fat. If you eat one cup of cooked beans a day, you can lower your cholesterol *by 10%!*

Beans are one of the best food sources of magnesium – a very important mineral. It can reduce angina and vascular spasms, help prevent congestive heart failure and Chronic Fatigue Syndrome.

Beans are rich in complex carbohydrates which can help to ease depression as well as improve sleep. Try eating some a couple of hours before bedtime. This will trigger the release of serotonin, the brain's natural sleep inducer.

Dried beans are rich in pectin as well as being high in fiber, which can help lower your risk of colon cancer. The high fiber they contain will fill you up with fewer calories.

Navy beans and pinto beans are good sources of calcium.

Pinto beans are high in folic acid. A deficiency of folic acid can make you more susceptible to blocked arteries, cancers of the lung, breast & esophagus, polyps that precede colon cancer and decreased mental functioning.

An iron deficiency can increase the risk of infection. Beans are good sources of iron.

Kidney beans and soybeans are an excellent source of Vitamin B-6. A deficiency of Vitamin B-6 makes one more prone to the signs of aging including declining mental abilities and infectious diseases.

Beets

Beets are rich in folic acid which can help to fight cervical cancer. A deficiency of folic acid can make you more susceptible to blocked arteries, cancers of the lung, breast & esophagus, polyps that precede colon cancer and decreased mental functioning.

Berries

Cranberries & blueberries can cut the risk of urinary tract infections by fifty per cent. It works by helping to eliminate bacteria from the urinary tract. Concentrated tannins found in cranberry juice prevent E. Coli bacteria from adhering to the urinary tract. E. Coli is the main culprit responsible for urinary infections.

Cranberries dilate the bronchial tubes during an asthma attack to help keep breathing normal.

Reduce the risk of cholesterol affecting your arteries by drinking cranberry juice.

Dried blueberries can help cure diarrhea.

Make tea from blackberry leaves. It contains plenty of tannin which helps fight cancer.

An elderberry and olive oil poultice will relieve hemorrhoid pain.

Blueberries and strawberries help to improve brain power.

Strawberries are high in Vitamin C and may help fight bronchitis and asthma. Reduced risk of breast, colon & prostate cancer have been linked to diets high in Vitamin C and is required to ward off many conditions of aging. People who get the most Vitamin C tend to have longer life spans. Plus it washes away the wastes and toxins eliminated during weight loss.

Vitamin C may reduce the risk of cancers of the mouth, esophagus and stomach as well as reducing the risk of heart disease, cataracts, raises good cholesterol (HDL), reduces bad cholesterol (LDL), improves the immune system, helps the common cold and fights depression

If you are taking a screening test for colon cancer, do not eat strawberries - or take Vitamin C tablets – for 3 days prior to the test as it can affect the accuracy of the test.

Remove coffee or tea stains from your teeth with strawberries. Crush the fruit, and gently rub the pulp onto your teeth, then rinse.

Raspberries and blackberries are also good sources for Vitamin C.

Broccoli

Broccoli is a great source of fiber. Adding this to your diet can help prevent colon cancer and improve cholesterol. The high fiber it contains will fill you up with fewer calories.

Broccoli is packed with chemicals that help to flush carcinogens from the body.

Heart patients using the blood thinner drug, Coumadin should be aware that foods high in Vitamin K –like broccoli – reduce the effectiveness of the drug.

Broccoli is a good source of Vitamin C and may help fight bronchitis and asthma. Reduced risk of breast, colon & prostate cancer have been linked to diets high in Vitamin C and is required to ward off many conditions of aging. People who get the most Vitamin C tend to have longer life spans.

Vitamin C may reduce the risk of cancers of the mouth, esophagus and stomach as well as reducing the risk of heart disease, cataracts, raises good cholesterol (HDL), reduces bad cholesterol (LDL), improves the immune system, helps the common cold and fights depression

Broccoli contains chemicals that speed up the removal of estrogen from the body which helps to inhibit breast cancer. Plus it washes away the wastes and toxins eliminated during weight loss.

Brussels Sprouts

Brussels Sprouts are packed with chemicals that help to flush carcinogens from the body.

The high fiber they contain will fill you up with fewer calories.

Cabbage

A note to new mothers: Place cabbage leaves in your bra. The cabbage draws out the milk and helps your to dry out quickly.

Cabbage is a great source of fiber. Adding this to your diet can help prevent colon cancer and improve cholesterol.

Cabbage is packed with chemicals that help to flush carcinogens from the body.

Raw cabbage is a good source of Vitamin C and may help fight bronchitis and asthma. Reduced risk of breast, colon & prostate cancer have been linked to diets high in Vitamin C and is required to ward off many conditions of aging. People who get the most Vitamin C tend to have longer life spans.

Vitamin C may reduce the risk of cancers of the mouth, esophagus and stomach as well as reducing the risk of heart disease, cataracts, raises good cholesterol (HDL), reduces bad cholesterol (LDL), improves the immune system, helps the common cold and fights depression Plus it washes away the wastes and toxins eliminated during weight loss.

Cabbage contains chemicals that speed up the removal of estrogen from the body which helps to inhibit breast cancer.

For painful joints caused by arthritis, try a poultice made from softened cabbage leaves covered with gauze.

To reduce the odor of cooked cabbage, put a half lemon into the pot.

Carrots

Carrots are rich in pectin, which can help lower your risk of colon cancer. A good source of beta-carotene, raw carrots – and especially carrot juice can also help protect against heart attack and stroke. Beta-Carotene works together with Vitamin C and E to maintain high antioxidant levels in the cells. It can help reduce the risk of cancer, heart disease, stroke, cataracts and night blindness.

Smokers can partially reverse the damage that leads to cancer by eating vegetables like carrots that are rich in beta-carotene. Beta-Carotene works together with Vitamin C and E to maintain high antioxidant levels in the cells. It can help reduce the risk of cancer, heart disease, stroke, cataracts and night blindness.

One of the best sources of cancer-fighting antioxidants is found in carrots. Eating just 1 carrot daily may decrease the risk of lung cancer by 50% even in previously heavy smokers.

You get 2.5 grams of fiber from a glass of carrot juice, which is more than you get from 2 whole apples.

Cantaloupe

A good source of beta-carotene, cantaloupe can help protect against heart attack and stroke. Beta-Carotene works together with Vitamin C and E to maintain high anti-oxidant levels in the cells. It can help reduce the risk of cancer, heart disease, stroke, cataracts and night blindness.

Cantaloupe is also rich in Vitamin C. Reduced risk of breast, colon & prostate cancer have been linked to diets high in Vitamin C. It may also help fight bronchitis and asthma. Vitamin C is required to ward off many conditions of aging. People who get the most Vitamin C tend to have longer life spans.

Vitamin C may reduce the risk of cancers of the mouth, esophagus and stomach as well as reducing the risk of heart disease, cataracts, raises good cholesterol (HDL), reduces bad cholesterol (LDL), improves the immune system, helps the common cold and fights depression Plus it washes away the wastes and toxins eliminated during weight loss.

If you are taking a screening test for colon cancer, do not eat cantaloupe - or take Vitamin C tablets – for 3 days prior to the test as it can affect the accuracy of the test.

One of the best sources of cancer-fighting antioxidants is found in cantaloupes.

Melons are incompatible with all foods especially grains, starches, cheese and fried food. The combination can cause stomach cramps, heartburn and indigestion.

Catnip

...Catnip tea is good for blood pressure. Take three to four tips and put them into two cups hot water and steep five minutes. He drinks it with his breakfast. Right now the catnip is a little bit hard to find, in the spring it's all over. You can find it all along the roadways when we go for a walk.

Cauliflower

Cauliflower is a great source of fiber. Adding this to your diet can help prevent colon cancer and improve cholesterol.

Cauliflower is packed with chemicals that help to flush carcinogens from the body.

Cauliflower is a good source of Vitamin C and may help fight bronchitis and asthma. Reduced risk of breast, colon & prostate cancer have been linked to diets high in Vitamin C and is required to ward off many conditions of aging. People who get the most Vitamin C tend to have longer life spans. Plus it washes away the wastes and toxins eliminated during weight loss.

Vitamin C may reduce the risk of cancers of the mouth, esophagus and stomach as well as reducing the risk of heart disease, cataracts, raises good cholesterol (HDL), reduces bad cholesterol (LDL), improves the immune system, helps the common cold and fights depression

Cauliflower contains chemicals that speed up the removal of estrogen from the body which helps to inhibit breast cancer.

Cayenne Pepper (Capsicum)

Hot peppers contain capsicum which may help keep carcinogens found in cigarette smoke from leading to lung cancer.

Small amounts of cayenne can improve digestion and appetite. It should be avoided by anyone suffering from hemorrhoids.

To relieve sinusitis, add a little cayenne pepper and garlic powder to a bowl of chicken soup. Drinking it will help to relieve the stuffy nose.

For headaches, squeeze half a lemon into a cup. Dice the peel and simmer it in 1 1/4 cup of water for 10 minutes. Strain into the cup. Add a pinch of cayenne pepper and 1/2 teaspoon of powdered ginger. Sweeten with maple syrup & drink.

An effective ointment made from capsicum is an effective treatment for muscle spasms and arthritis. It is also used to relieve pain from shingles and surgical scars.

Celery

Eating plenty of raw celery can help protect you from stomach cancer.

Celery juice can help you to lose weight.

Chamomile

Before refrigeration was invented, meat was immersed in an infusion of chamomile to prevent spoiling. Chamomile is known as *The Plant Physician* because plants placed near it that are dying are revived.

Chamomile is an annual that usually reseeds itself, so you may not have to plant it every year. There are two types of chamomile, German and Roman. They can both be used in remedies, but German chamomile is most commonly used. There are also two spellings – chamomile and camomile. Both are correct.

The fragrant flowers of the chamomile plant are often used as teas and extracts. It is most commonly used to relieve an upset stomach, menstrual cramps and to aid digestion.

Those prone to hay fever may suffer a mild allergic reaction such as skin rash or wheezing. It can cause a severe reaction in those allergic to ragweed. The use of chamomile can cause contact dermatitis. It should be avoided by pregnant women as it stimulates the uterus.

Chamomile tea aids digestion and eases upset stomach. It helps to relax the stomach muscles and bring you relief. A possible side effect of chamomile is an allergic reaction such as a skin rash or wheezing in those with ragweed allergies.

Chamomile tea has anti-spasmodic properties and will relieve menstrual cramps.

Corn

High fiber foods like corn will fill you up with fewer calories.

If you are having problems going to sleep at night, you may find it helpful to include foods high in complex carbohydrates – like corn - in your evening meal. This will trigger the release of serotonin, the brain's natural sleep inducer.

Corn forms a gas producing compound when refrigerated. The more often they are thawed, reheated and re-refrigerated, the more potent they become. So don't reheat more than you plan to eat in one sitting.

Echinacea (Purple Cone flower)

Echinacea can help many ailments including, influenza, candida, strep throat, staph infections, pelvic inflammatory disease, infected wounds and herpes.

Eggplant

If you have to undergo surgery that requires anesthesia, stay away from foods in the nightshade family –like eggplant– at least 3 days prior to your surgery. These foods interfere with the body's ability to break down the anesthetic.

... Eggplant grows so slow and my husband drinks eggplant juice. It's a natural thing that helps regulate blood pressure. Chop into one-half inch cubes and put in a glass gallon jar. Fill with good water not spigot water and leave set for 4 days. Drain the juice off and he drinks the juice. Keep refrigerated up to 2 weeks. It is dark in color and doesn't have much of a smell. Storebought eggplant doesn't get as dark. I wish those eggplant would grow a little faster!...

Garlic

Folklore says that garlic sprouted from Satan's left footprint when he left the Garden of Eden.

One of the earliest labor strikes known to man is connected with garlic. Egyptians fed their slaves garlic to boost their strength and endurance while building the pyramids. When the garlic was withheld, the slaves responded by refusing to work.

In medieval France, *The Legend of Four Thieves* is widely known. There were four thieves who were hired to bury plague victims. They protected themselves by drinking a mixture of wine vinegar and crushed garlic. Since the 18th century, this remedy has been sold throughout France.

Garlic has solid scientific research that shows it can help to prevent certain cancers including breast cancer and stomach cancer as well as lower cholesterol, prevent blood clots and ward off aging. Over 1,000 scientific papers have been published on the healing properties of garlic.

The National Cancer Institute launched a five-year study concerning garlic's anti-cancer effects. The health benefits of garlic are due to its natural compound, allicin. Allicin is produced when the enzyme allinase reacts with another natural substance allin. To insure the effectiveness of garlic, the conversion of allin to allicin must occur within the digestive tract. Allicin is present in uncooked garlic only. It is destroyed during the cooking process. Dosage is 400 mg. daily or one average size garlic clove.

Using too much salt? Cut back by using more garlic!

Garlic can be produced every year simply by planting cloves you've grown or purchased at the grocery store.

Garlic can cause burning of the mouth, esophagus and stomach as well as nausea, sweating and light-headedness. It shouldn't be used by those taking anti-clotting drugs or people with clotting disorders. Garlic reduces blood sugar and will have a negative impact on glucose control.

Garlic is the top-selling herbal remedy in the country and has been proven to lower cholesterol, reduce blood pressure and even has cancer-fighting properties. The active ingredient, allicin is present only in uncooked garlic. Most of allicin is destroyed during cooking.

Eating garlic at least once a week can help to reduce your risk of colon cancer as garlic contains chemicals that stimulate cancer-fighting immune cells.

The Journal of The American Cancer Institute reported a Chinese study on 1600 people. Those who ate the most garlic, onions, chives, leeks and shallots had 60% fewer cases of stomach cancer than those who ate lesser amounts of these foods.

Studies show that cholesterol can be reduced by as much as 15% with garlic. Eat 2 cloves a day or at least 300 mg. of a deodorized supplement.

Selenium is a trace mineral and a powerful antioxidant found in garlic. It fights cancer, reduces heart disease, fights viruses by increasing the immune system function & relieves anxiety.

Cold sore? Cut a clove of garlic in half & rub the juicy side on the sore.

To relieve sinusitis, add a little garlic powder and cayenne pepper to a bowl of chicken soup. Drinking it will help to relieve the stuffy nose. Any soup flavored with garlic will help to loosen nasal congestion.

Prevent garlic breath by mincing the garlic and adding it to yogurt thus eliminating chewing the garlic. Other garlic breath remedies are: suck on a lemon, chew on an orange peel, eat lime sherbet, chew or swallow some coffee beans, drink a glass of milk, chew or swallow some anise seeds, drink some red wine, chew on a mint leaf, suck on a cinnamon stick or chew or swallow whole cloves.

If you eat a lot of garlic, the smell of garlic may come out your pores. Try adding the herb lavender to your bath water.

Juniper

Juniper is a mild diuretic and will help with monthly bloating or upset stomach. It should not be used by anyone with kidney problems.

Lavender

A great massage oil for sore muscles & joints can be easily made by putting lavender flowers and eucalyptus leaves into a bottle of almond oil. Let stand 2-3 weeks before use.

To soothe a baby to sleep, put a few drops of the essential oil of lavender into water in a vaporizer.

Can't get to sleep? Try a cup of lavender tea.

Lemon Balm

Lemon balm is mentioned in *Homer's Odyssey* – a poem over 2700 years old! Shakespeare also names it in several of his plays. Roman naturalist writer, Pliny the Elder, urged soldiers going into battle to attach a sprig of lemon balm to their swords help with wounds.

The same healing properties that exist in honey and royal jelly are included in lemon balm. A cup of lemon balm tea will help calm nervousness and anxiety. As a compress, it can relieve the pain of gout. As an ointment, it can be used for insect bites or to repel insects.

If you love the taste of lemon, the uses for lemon balm leaves are endless. Add the fresh leaves to green salads or fruit salads to add a lovely flavor. If you are tea lover, lemon balm and honey makes a delightful brew.

Mint

The origin of mint lies in Greek mythology. Persephone, wife of Hades discovered that her husband was in love with Menthe, a beautiful nymph. She was so jealous, that she transformed the nymph into a plant – now known as mint.

There are references to mint in the Bible. It seems that the plant was so valuable, that the Pharisees demanded that tithes be paid with mint.

It is believed that negative energy can be banished by washing down the walls in your home with a diluted mint infusion. The fragrance of mint is also said to help writers.

Mint is a perennial, and there are many varieties. Some of the more common ones are peppermint, spearmint, bergamot (orange mint) and pennyroyal. Be sure to plant the different varieties of mint well away from each other as cross-pollination will weaken the flavors of each plant.

Mint's antibiotic properties make it a good remedy against infection. A mixture of oil and either crushed peppermint leaves or crushed spearmint leaves can be massaged into the affected area for relief from muscle pain and migraine headaches.

Peppermint is a treatment for indigestion, hiccups and flatulence when used as a tea or essential oil. As an ointment, it can be rubbed under the nose to ease throat and chest congestion

Peppermint can be irritating to the stomach. Those prone to heartburn may suffer from chest pain following a cup of peppermint tea. By relaxing the valve near the stomach's entrance, the menthol can allow digestive acids into the esophagus.

Note: Never give peppermint to infants or toddlers as the menthol can make them feel as though they are choking.

Note: The essential oil of peppermint and pure menthol are poisonous and should never be taken internally.

The essential oil of spearmint can be sprinkled onto a clean cloth and inhaled to bring relief from a cold.

Spearmint can be irritating to the stomach.

Pennyroyal should never be taken internally as it can destroy the liver and has caused at least one death.

The best way to grow mint is in large flower pots pushed down so it is level with the ground because mint will <u>really</u> spread.

Onions

Promising studies show that people who eat a lot of onions are less likely to develop cancer. Onions – as well as scallions and chives contain chemicals that stimulate cancer-fighting immune cells.

The Journal of The American Cancer Institute reported a Chinese study on 1600 people. Those who ate the most onions, chives, garlic, leeks and shallots had 60% fewer cases of stomach cancer than those who ate lesser amounts of these foods.

Onions – as well as chives, scallions, leeks & shallots may help to control asthma attacks.

Oregano

For ringworm, rub oil of oregano on the area twice a day.

Folklore's name for oregano is joy of the mountain. It made its debut in this country after World War II when servicemen brought it back from Italy and Greece. Its most common use is in Italian cooking.

Oregano is a perennial, the most common of which is also known as Wild Marjoram – not to be confused with Marjoram. It is usually used in its dry form but it can be frozen. Simply put oregano leaves in an ice cube tray and fill with water. When they are frozen, transfer them to freezer bags. They will bring a marvelous flavor to soups, stews and sauces.

For a toothache put a few drops of oregano oil directly on the tooth to help relieve the pain.

Parsley

Parsley's earliest use as a garnish can be traced back to the Roman Empire. It was placed on the plate with the food to protect against contamination. It was also fed to race horses as it was believed to provide extra stamina. In the Bible St. Peter referred to it as a sacred plant.

It is said to be bad luck to give parsley away - or to receive it. Moving it is equally unlucky.

Parsley is technically a biennial, but because of its inconsistent growing pattern it should be treated as an annual and planted each year. Parsley can be frozen. Actually, parsley has more flavor when frozen than when used after it is dried.

Since parsley is a good source of chlorophyll, it is good for bad breath. Dip parsley sprigs into white vinegar and chew. This is considered the best remedy for garlic breath.

Freshen your dog's breath by adding fresh parsley to your dog's food.

Although parsley is most widely known for its uses in the kitchen, it has medicinal qualities as well. It can be used as a poultice to relieve the pain of sprains, bruises and insect bites.

As a tea, parsley leaves can be used to treat coughs, menstrual cramps, rheumatism, kidney stones, urinary infections, cystitis and jaundice. A 1/2 cup of parsley provides two-thirds of the daily requirement of Vitamin C, which is twice as much as one-cup of pineapple does.

Parsley is high in the mineral zinc which makes it good for men's reproductive health.

Parsley seeds are poisonous and should never be taken internally. Never use parsley if you are pregnant or have a kidney inflammation.

If using parsley frequently medicinally, you should eat foods high in potassium, like bananas. Parsley is considered a diuretic which depletes the body's supply of potassium.

Don't attempt to pick wild parsley as it resembles other toxic plants.

Parsley is Mother Nature's way of freshening your breath. But did you know that its diuretic action can help to relieve urinary tract infections.

If you suffer from cystitis, try drinking parsley tea. The tea is also good for indigestion and gas pains.

Pears

Pears are rich in pectin, which can help lower your risk of colon cancer.

Pears also have potassium that helps to lower blood pressure.

Symptoms of a potassium deficiency are:
Loss of mental alertness & memory
Increased mental & muscle fatigue
Sensitive to cold – cold hands & feet
Corns & calluses are more likely to appear
Increased constipation
You get sick more often – catch colds easily
Loss of appetite – nausea & vomiting
Slow healing of cuts & bruises
Itchy skin
Increased tooth decay
Appearance of pimples
Eyelid & mouth twitching
Nighttime leg cramps
Hard to relax
Difficulty sleeping
Soreness in the joints

One mid-size pear has as much fiber as 2 slices of whole-wheat bread.

Foods sweetened with fructose (fruit, soda & juice – especially pear & apple juice) and sorbitol (sugarless gum &

candy) may produce intestinal gas. Spread your intake over the entire day so your system isn't hit all at once.

Are you a pear? Pear shaped women carry more weight in the hips and thighs and have a lesser risk of heart disease.

Peppers

Vitamin C is required to ward off many conditions of aging. People who get the most Vitamin C tend to have longer life spans. Plus it washes away the wastes and toxins eliminated during weight loss.

Vitamin C may reduce the risk of cancers of the mouth, esophagus and stomach as well as reducing the risk of heart disease, cataracts, raises good cholesterol (HDL), reduces bad cholesterol (LDL), improves the immune system, helps the common cold and fights depression.

Sweet peppers are high in Vitamin C and may help fight bronchitis and asthma.

Green and red peppers are also good sources of Vitamin C. Reduced risk of breast, colon & prostate cancer have been linked to diets high in Vitamin C.

If you are taking a screening test for colon cancer, do not eat peppers - or take Vitamin C tablets – for 3 days prior to the test as it can affect the accuracy of the test.

Raw sweet red bell peppers are a good food source of Beta-Carotene. Beta Carotene works together with Vitamin C and E to maintain high antioxidant levels in the cells. It can help reduce the risk of cancer, heart disease, stroke, cataracts and night blindness.

Potatoes

Potatoes are an excellent source of Vitamin B-6. If you are deficient in this vitamin, you are more likely to get headaches.

Potatoes are rich in complex carbohydrates which can help to ease depression as well as improve sleep. Try eating some a couple of hours before bedtime. This will trigger the release of serotonin, the brain's natural sleep inducer.

Soups made from things like potatoes satisfy your hunger because they are loaded with carbohydrates. The body converts them quickly into glucose which raises blood sugar levels and cuts back hunger.

If you are having problems going to sleep at night, you may find it helpful to include foods high in complex carbohydrates – like potatoes - in your evening meal.

Potatoes also contain starch which can help diarrhea.

If you have to undergo surgery that requires anesthesia, stay away from foods in the nightshade family –like potatoes – at least 3 days prior to your surgery. These foods interfere with the body's ability to break down the anesthetic.

Mashed potatoes may help relieve heartburn.

If you accidentally use too much salt when making soups or stews, add a cut, peeled raw potato. Cook for 10-15 minutes, and the potato will absorb the extra salt.

Radishes

Radishes are packed with chemicals that help to flush carcinogens from the body.

Rose Hips

A storehouse of Vitamin C is found in rose hips which come from rosa rugosa. The rugosa blossoms into a rose with a single petal. Once the petal falls off, you can harvest the fruit – which is the hips. Make rose hips marmalade by soaking clean rose hips for 2 hours in cold water. Simmer for 2 hours and strain. Add 1 cup brown sugar to 1 cup of the rose hips. Boil until thick, then pour into sterilized glasses & seal as usual.

Rosemary

Rosemary tea will enhance circulation.

Make an invigorating bath from Rosemary leaves to help treat circulatory problems.

St. John's Wort

Studies show that St. John's Wort (Hypericum) improves symptoms of mild depression without the side effects of drugs like Prozac.

Be sure to avoid red wine, strong cheese, sausage and soy beans including fermented soy beans and soy bean paste when taking St. John's Wort or there may be serious side effects. These foods contain a high amount of the chemical, tyramine which can cause a dangerous rise in blood pressure that can be fatal. Never take St. John's Wort along with prescription drugs.

Sage

A gargle of sage oil and water relieves sore throats and inflammation of the mouth caused by colds or flu.

Help relieve hot flashes by drinking sage tea. The tea also helps clear a dry cough.

Spinach

A good source of beta-carotene, spinach can help protect against heart attack and stroke. Beta-Carotene works together with Vitamin C and E to maintain high antioxidant levels in the cells. It can help reduce the risk of cancer, heart disease, stroke, cataracts and night blindness. Spinach is also a good source of calcium.

Smokers can partially reverse the damage that leads to cancer by eating vegetables like spinach that is rich in beta-carotene. It also helps to improve brain power.

The British Medical Journal found that spinach is closely linked to preventing cataracts in women. This may be because of the high amount of Beta-Carotene in spinach.

Eating just 1 cup of spinach daily may decrease the risk of lung cancer by 50% even in previously heavy smokers.

Heart patients using the blood thinner drug, Coumadin should be aware that foods high in Vitamin K –like spinach– reduce the effectiveness of the drug.

Sweet Potatoes

A good source of beta-carotene, sweet potatoes can also help protect against heart attack and stroke. Beta-Carotene works together with Vitamin C and E to maintain high anti-oxidant levels in the cells. It can help reduce the risk of cancer, heart disease, stroke, cataracts and night blindness.

Smokers can partially reverse the damage that leads to cancer by eating vegetables like sweet potatoes that are rich in beta-carotene.

Sweet potatoes are a good source of Vitamin C. Reduced risk of breast, colon & prostate cancer have been linked to diets high in Vitamin C. It may also help fight bronchitis and asthma. Plus it washes away the wastes and toxins eliminated during weight loss.

Vitamin C is required to ward off many conditions of aging. People who get the most Vitamin C tend to have longer life spans. Vitamin C may reduce the risk of cancers of the mouth, esophagus and stomach as well as reducing the risk of heart disease, cataracts, raises good cholesterol (HDL), reduces bad cholesterol (LDL), improves the immune system, helps the common cold and fights depression.

If you are taking a screening test for colon cancer, do not eat sweet potatoes - or take Vitamin C tablets – for 3 days prior to the test as it can affect the accuracy of the test.

If you have to undergo surgery that requires anesthesia, stay away from foods in the nightshade family –like sweet potatoes – at least 3 days prior to your surgery. These foods interfere with the body's ability to break down the anesthetic.

Sweet potatoes are an excellent source of Vitamin B-6. A deficiency of Vitamin B-6 makes one more prone to the signs of aging including declining mental abilities and infectious diseases.

Squash

Soups made from things like squash satisfy your hunger because they are loaded with carbohydrates. The body converts them quickly into glucose, which raises blood sugar levels and cuts back hunger.

Try eating some a couple of hours before bedtime. This will trigger the release of serotonin, the brain's natural sleep inducer.

Thyme

During World War I thyme was used as an antiseptic. In 17th century England, thyme was used to prevent the Black Plague. The ancient Greeks used it for purification. Folklore has it that if wild thyme is growing, a powerful source of earth energy is nearby.

Thyme is a perennial commonly used in French, Cajun and Creole cooking. There are many varieties of this hardy plant, but Wild English Thyme has the strongest medicinal properties.

Thyme is one of the best sources of thymol. This antiseptic compound is soothing to the stomach and can help to prevent blood clots internally that cause heart attacks.

As a tea it can help reduce a hangover, fight bronchitis, pneumonia, coughs and respiratory inflammations.

Thyme's powerful antispasmodic properties make it a good cough remedy. Make a thyme-honey syrup with 3 tablespoons dried thyme leaves (not powdered thyme) and 1 pint boiling water. Steep until cool. Strain and add 1 cup honey. Stir and keep refrigerated It will keep for several months. 1 teaspoon hourly will help relieve a cough.

Use the fresh or dried herb as the essential oil of thyme should not be taken internally.

Thyme tea fights bronchitis, coughs and other respiratory ailments. It will also relieve a sore throat by gargling with the tea.

Tomatoes

Those who eat raw tomatoes at least seven times a week can reduce their risk of several types of cancer in half – including stomach and pancreatic cancer.

Tomatoes are high in Vitamin C and may help fight bronchitis and asthma. Vitamin C is required to ward off many conditions of aging. People who get the most Vitamin C tend to have longer life spans. Plus it washes away the wastes and toxins eliminated during weight loss.

Vitamin C may reduce the risk of cancers of the mouth, esophagus and stomach as well as reducing the risk of heart disease, cataracts, raises good cholesterol (HDL), reduces bad cholesterol (LDL), improves the immune system, helps the common cold and fights depression.

Tomato juice contains twice the Vitamin C of apple juice, is low in calories and contains the powerful antioxidant lycopene, a red pigment known to help protect against cancer.

If you are taking a screening test for colon cancer, do not eat tomatoes - or take Vitamin C tablets – for 3 days prior to the test as it can affect the accuracy of the test.

One of the best sources of cancer-fighting antioxidants is found in tomatoes.

Soups made from things like tomatoes satisfy your hunger because they are loaded with carbohydrates. The body converts them quickly into glucose, which raises blood sugar levels and cuts back hunger.

If you have to undergo surgery that requires anesthesia, stay away from foods in the nightshade family –like tomatoes – at least 3 days prior to your surgery. These foods interfere with the body's ability to break down the anesthetic.

Violets

As well as being beautiful, violet blossoms are edible. They are three times higher in Vitamin C ounce per ounce as oranges. They also contain Vitamin A. If you ever have the chance, try violet syrup!

Watermelon

An iron deficiency can increase the risk of infection. Watermelon has more iron than any other fruit.

Watermelon is a good source of Beta-Carotene. Beta Carotene works together with Vitamin C and E to maintain high antioxidant levels in the cells. It can help reduce the risk of cancer, heart disease, stroke, cataracts and night blindness.

Watermelon is one of the richest source of lycopene, a red pigment known to help protect against cancer.

Witch Hazel

Try Witch Hazel leaves for sore throats, hemorrhoids, and eye ailments. It is also helpful to rub on the eyebrow area to help numb the pain before tweezing.

Herb Garden

Most people plant an herb garden because they enjoy cooking with them. Sweet basil makes great pesto, mint and chamomile are wonderful teas, tarragon is for vinegar and parsley enhances many dishes.

Many herbs have medicinal uses, but the effectiveness of the herb has much to do with the soil. Plants grown in virgin soil will contain a much higher medicinal value than those grown in poor, nutritionally depleted soil.

Your herb garden can be as easy as a few flowerpots on your windowsill or as complex as a full-size garden in your yard.

Planting your own herb garden

Never begin planting your herb garden with the dirt you find outside. If you plant your herbs in poor soil, the end result will be poor quality herbs. Ideally you will make a mixture of equal parts potting soil and peat moss plus two parts vermiculite. The vermiculite holds water and makes it easier for the new plants to grow. All three ingredients can be purchased from your local garden center.

Some seeds need to be softened before they are planted by soaking them in water. Others may need frozen or refrigerated. Once planted, some seeds need darkness to grow while others need light. Some seeds are easy to maintain – just plant them and they will grow. Other seeds need bottom heat, which can be easily accomplished by simply placing the seed tray on top of your refrigerator.

The seeds have to germinate before they can be potted. Pay particular attention to the germination time required for the seed you are growing. Once they begin to sprout, they need at least 12 hours of light every day. Be careful not to place them in direct sunlight. Once the plants are at least 3 inches high, they need to be placed outside for a few hours every day to get them used to the elements. The ideal conditions are 65-70 degrees under a tree or other shady spot. If the temperature is below 60 degrees, place them in the garage.

Some herb gardens are created to fit into a certain theme. Someone in the clergy may want to plant only biblical herbs. History buffs may want a Shakespeare garden. Some may want a garden strictly for creating potpourri and dried bouquets. Others care only about color.

If you're looking to plant a more fragrant garden, choose from these herbs: chamomile, catmint, curry, dill, fennel, hyssop, lavender, lemon balm, lemon verbena, oregano, rosemary, sage, mint, pennyroyal, basil, thyme, sweet marjoram, pelargoniums or valerian.

Invasive herbs spread almost in a blink of an eye and are very difficult to control or contain in an open garden. Some of the more common of these include: Artemisa, Bible leaf, Comfrey, Fennel, German Chamomile (Matricaria recutita), St. John's Wort, Tansy, Violet and Yarrow. If you want to plant any of these, use a container.

Chapter 6:

Garden Remedies for your Home

...Gardening is the responsibility of women and small children. Men and boys do the field work, but women will help during planting and harvesting...

The National Aeronautics and Space Administration (NASA) did research studies on indoor contaminants. They found that indoor pollution comes from almost everything including furniture, drapes, carpet, plastic, paper towels, facial tissue, ink, insulation, paint, office machines, etc. etc. These contaminants can cause sore throats, stuffy nose, headaches, nausea, pimples and watery eyes to name a few.

Their studies further discovered that there are five common houseplants that can substantially reduce the toxic level of chemicals in the air we breathe. These plants are Chinese Evergreen, Golden Pothos, Peace Lily, Spider plant and Weeping Fig.

NASA states that one plant can remove up to 87% of the pollutants in each hundred square foot area!

Cleaning & Deodorizing

A decoction of the essential oils of thyme and alcohol make a strong disinfectant. It is an antiseptic smell that was used in ancient Egypt for embalming.

Lemon balm makes a great furniture polish. Rub the leaves on the wood and let the oil in the leaves work its magic.

Blend the essential oils of roses and lavender with water and use for cleaning and freshening indoors.

The essential oils of rosewood, oregano and thyme can kill bacteria, even those that cause pneumonia. NEVER take essential oils internally. Get yourself an aromatherapy diffuser and experiment with different scents.

Hang mint from the ceiling on hot, humid days to freshen the air with a scent of coolness. Countries with hot climates use this practice.

Scent the air of your home by placing cinnamon sticks, orange peel, lemon peel, cloves or any combination into a pan of water on your stove. Simmer slowly and add water as needed.

Make a blend of your favorite scents and put them into some old pantyhose. Tie it at the end and hang in a heating vent.

Put a few drops of vanilla extract or your favorite essence on a cotton ball Put them in a corner then vacuum them up. This will make your room and carpets smell nice. Replace them each time you vacuum.

Use scented candles throughout your home. They fill the air with fragrance and make your home look more inviting.

Leave a bowl of lemon juice or vinegar out to absorb odors in a room.

Freshen your carpets by combining a box of baking soda with 1 cup of lavender, 1 cup of pennyroyal and 1 tablespoon of crushed coriander seeds. Sprinkle on the carpet and let set overnight then vacuum.

Decorating

Dried basil can be used in wreaths. It can also be combined with calendula.

Dried chive flowers look nice in dried wreaths & arrangements.

Sweet basil leaves can be used in decorating to fill your home with a wonderful aroma.

Dried flowers or leaves of Angelica, bay, scented geranium, hyssop and rosemary can be made into sweet-smelling swags to drape over doorways or mantles.

Dried arrangements can be attractive by using the seed pods of bittersweet, iris, lily, poppy, delphinium or Chinese lantern.

If it is pressed flowers that you like, these will work best: bleeding heart, chrysanthemum, clematis, cone flower, crocus, dahlia, freesia, geranium, heather, larkspur, lobelia, English primrose and tulips.

Dried herbs look pretty tied in bundles and hung from wooden drying racks.

Try stenciling a favorite saying onto an old piece of wood. Then hang some dried herb bundles from it for a delightful accent to your home.

Press herb leaves or flowers between sheets of blotting paper or newspaper with a flower press. A heavy book will work too. When your leaves are dry, frame a nice arrangement as a print to hang in your home or give as a gift.

Place dried rose petals in baskets, jars or lamp bases. This is a good idea for those roses that came from someone special or have sentimental value.

Be sure to keep your candles away from drafts. They will drip less and last longer.

Add some fun to your table. Use tomatoes, apples, pumpkins, oranges or whatever as candlesticks. Just cut out an opening and insert the candle.

Fishing Tips

Rub anise oil on your bait to attract fish.

Houseplants

Use the foam peanuts commonly using in packages in the bottom of your plants. It is light weight and it drains water well.

To keep cats away from houseplants, try putting pine cones around the plant.

Cover the dirt in your potted plants with seashells. It looks pretty and will keep your pet out of the dirt.

Once your plant starts to grow, fertilize it once a month. It is better to underwater than to overwater, but ideally use a soil tester. Keep your plants in a cool room but away from drafts or direct heat.

To keep pests away from houseplants, put a small strip from a flea collar in the dirt.

To dust dried flowers just use an empty turkey baster and blow off the dust.

Clean silk flowers with a plastic bag & some salt. Just shake & they're clean. You want to do this outside or over a sink.

Stick a clove of garlic into the soil around your houseplants leaving the tip of the clove sticking up above the dirt. This will eliminate the insects.

Mildew

Get rid of mildew in the basement and bathroom with a strong infusion of chives.

Prepare an infusion of chamomile and use it in the bathtub or shower to banish mildew.

Pomanders

Make your own fragrant potpourri balls. Spread white glue over a styrofoam ball and roll it in potpourri. Fill in any hole with additional glue and potpourri. Use them in a basket to add a soft fragrance to the air.

When the fragrance begins to wane, add a couple drops of essential oil.

Potpourri

A gentle way to scent the air is with potpourri. Make them with fresh herbs to make your home smell like a sweet meadow.

Make small potpourri sachets to add a pleasing aroma to drawers, suitcases, cars or any small place.

Try making potpourri with dried orange, lemon or lime slices, dried orange, lemon or lime peel, dried pomegranates, dried cranberries, dried blueberries, cinnamon sticks, cloves & pine cones.

For citrus potpourri – use lemon basil. For added color in your potpourri, use purple basil.

Sweet clover is commonly used in potpourri because of its delicate fragrance. Sweet smelling potpourri can also be made from lavender, sweet violet, sweet marjoram, roses, peppermint, orange bergamot mint, lemon verbena, lemon balm, fennel, borage chamomile and bergamot.

Marjoram is known as a gentle, calming herbs and was believed to be the favorite of Aphrodite, the goddess of love. There are two varieties of Marjoram: Sweet Marjoram and Wild Marjoram – which is more commonly known as oregano.

Marjoram has no medicinal value. It is used to scent perfume and soaps as well as potpourri and sachets.

Ancient Greeks referred to it as *"joy of the mountains"*. Legend has it that you would dream of your future spouse if you sprinkled yourself with Marjoram before going to sleep. Greek brides and grooms wore a crown formed from Marjoram.

A good combination for potpourri for the kitchen is rosemary, sage, thyme, bay and cloves.

...for the study combine pine, bayberry, basil, mint, rosemary, and juniper. They are all believed to improve mental clarity.

...for the bedroom combine sweet flowers like carnations and lavender. You could add roses and cardamom which are believed to be aphrodisiacs.

Note: Pennyroyal and mountain mint should not be used if you are pregnant.

Topiaries

Make a topiary to decorate any room in your home!

❖ Make a pomander. Cover a wooden dowel with colorful, shiny ribbon and insert it into the pomander. Use any container you like as your base and cover with moss.

❖ Cover a wooden dowel with moss and insert it into a styrofoam cone that is also covered with moss. Cover the cone with any material you desire to make a tree. You can use basil leaves, rose hips, dried rose petals, cinnamon sticks, garlic, seeds, dried flowers and herbs or any material you find pleasing to the eye. Use any container you like as your base and cover with moss or other material.

❖ Instead of a wooden dowel, use a sturdy twig. Be creative and come up with your own ideas.

Lawn & Garden Furniture

Keep outdoor plastic furniture clean by applying car wax each season. This will also help to prevent fading.

Scratches on wrought iron furniture? Just use a black crayon and blend it in.

If they really look bad and you want to repaint them, don't use a brush. Use a sponge instead. It's easier and quicker too.

...The beverage with meals was always water. We never had coffee growing up because my dad had ulcers. Sometimes during hot days we gave the men ice tea or lemonade, but I always drank water. I still do. In the morning I drink a cup of hot water with nothing in it...

Chapter 7:

What to do about Insects

See Laura's slug remedy and pest remedy in Chapter 3 under Pests.

As a bug-hater at heart, I can understand the emotion of the gardener with the goal to eliminate each and every insect. But even I realize that there really are good bugs. We should never aim for 100 percent pest-free plants in a backyard garden.

The widespread use of pesticides over the years has certainly left its mark on our world. Contaminated ground water, depleted topsoil, loss of minerals in the soil and a link to cancer are all a result of the extensive use of toxins.

There are many alternatives to pesticides when fighting the pests that threaten your garden. For instance:

You can make an effective spray against insects that is all natural. Strong herbs like garlic, parsley and tansy are normally avoided by insects. Grind the leaves of the herb plant and plus a small amount of liquid soap and water. Let the mixture sit for about 30 minutes, then transfer into a spray bottle and apply to plants you want to protect.

Hot pepper spray can also be effective in repelling insects. Cut about four or five hot peppers into chunks – seeds and all. Grind the peppers in your blender, then add a little liquid soap and water. Let the mixture sit for about 30 minutes, then transfer into a spray bottle. Apply to plants as needed.

Natural bug spray can be made by boiling 4 large onions and 4 heads of garlic in 1 gallon of water for approximately 45 minutes. When it is cool, put it in a spray bottle and spray your vegetable garden. It is safe and has no odor.

Sometimes soap or even water can be an effective spray against garden pests. Fill a spray bottle with liquid soap and water and apply to your plants. Sometimes the pests can be knocked out with a steady stream of water from your garden hose.

Things like beer, ammonia, baby powder, dried ginger, liquid soap, hot pepper spray, garlic, castor oil and more can be used effectively. See Chapter 3 for details.

Too much pesticide is not healthy for any of us. It isn't good for the gardener, it isn't good for the environment and it isn't good for the beneficial insects. Too many chemicals can also create pesticide-resistant pests. This occurs in the same way as a person's overuse of antibiotics can lead to a super infection resistant to any medication.

Of all the synthetic herbicides on the market, Roundup is the least harmful. If you are allergic to poison ivy, this is a good product to try.

Cultivate your garden, and keep an eye on your plants. But at the same time learn to develop some degree of tolerance for pests. Use natural alternatives to pest control, and use pesticides only as a last resort.

Here are some helpful hints:

- Make sure that you don't do your planting at the same time that the problem insect is emerging. Do a little research to learn the natural enemies of what you are planting.
- Rotate your crops to interrupt the life of harmful organisms, and don't repeat for three to five years. Besides the benefit of keeping plant diseases and the insect population under control, crop rotation helps to replenish the soil of vital nutrients.
- Interrupt the spread of insects by staggering your plants By planting one row of beans, one row of tomatoes, etc. you are making it easy for the bugs to just go down the buffet line.
- Keep your garden weeded to destroy the pest's habitat. This is the area that usually does us in.
- Use biological control. Find out the natural predators for what you are planting and use that information.

In the late 1800's this pest - the cottony-cushion scale, seriously threatened the citrus industry in California. It had no natural enemies, and was destroying the groves. The United States Department of Agriculture's team of entomologists discovered the bedalia beetle in Australia. It looks very similar to the ladybug, and it preyed on the scale. Within two years the threat was removed. The bedalia beetle keeps the scales in check to this day.

- Erect border plants.
- Try natural repellents.
- Use botanical insecticides. They come from plants and are readily available.

Make your own natural liquid fertilizer. Place large comfrey leaves in a plastic garbage can until it is half full. Then add water to the top. Let it soak for 3 weeks until the leaves have rotted. Mix equal parts of this base liquid with fresh water and pour it around the roots of your plants.

Here is a list of common garden insects and other critters along with some remedies to help keep them away from your garden.

Ants

Rub a lemon balm leaf on the table to repel ants.

Mint deters ants.

Repel ants by sprinkling coffee grounds around the opening where they are entering your house.

Keep ants away from your picnic by cutting off the tops of old bleach bottles and filling them with water. Place under the legs of your picnic table. Since the ants can't cross water, your picnic is safe.

Keep bugs out of your drink when picnicking with aluminum foil. Just cover the glass with foil and poke your straw through.

Aphids

Keep aphids away from roses, lettuce & peas, by planting garlic. The best time to plant garlic is September, October & November.

Interplant chives, anise, coriander, nasturtiums or petunias to repel aphids.

Spray a soapy water solution on broccoli to stop aphids.

Since aphids are attracted to the color yellow, try filling bright yellow plastic plates with soapy water. Place these at the base of the plants you want to protect

Bees

Bees love the lemon balm plant so much so that they will supposedly never leave their hive if there is a lemon balm plant nearby.

Bees love a lot of the plants used in butterfly gardens. So if you are allergic to bee stings, you may want to avoid planting a butterfly garden.

To enjoy your picnic without the bees, try hanging a piece of sausage on a string a little ways away from the table.

Take a 2 liter bottle of regular soda with about 2″ of soda remaining. Arrange these near your outdoor picnic. The bees are attracted to the soda and will fly into the bottle, but they can't get out.

Birds

Movement scares birds. Try using a child's pinwheel or colorful plastic streamers. Less attractive but effective are aluminum pie tins strung on fishing line between wooden stakes.

To keep birds away, lay a large plastic snake in your garden or use a decoy of a great horned owl.

Scare away birds and animals from your garden by placing aluminum pie pans tied with string in your garden. The noise will scare the pests away.

Cover strawberry and raspberry bushes with old lace curtains to keep the birds away.

Cats & Dogs

To keep cats and dogs out of your garden, sprinkle hot cayenne pepper in the area you would like them to stay out of. Once they taste it, they will go elsewhere.

Mix 1 tablespoon of Lysol disinfectant into 1 gallon of water. Sprinkle around the border of your garden to keep pets away.

Interplant the herb, rue to discourage cats or simply scatter the dried leaves.

To keep cats out of your garden, spread a mixture of orange peel and old coffee grounds.

Plant pot marigolds to keep dogs out of the garden.

Keep dogs from digging in your garden by sprinkling cayenne pepper around the area.

Plant calendula around evergreens to keep dogs away.

Deer

Protect young trees from deer by wrapping the trunk of the tree with aluminum foil. Wrap it about 3/4 of the way up the trunk.

Earwigs

These nasty looking guys like cool, dark places, decaying matter and mulch. To trap them, use an empty tuna fish can filled with beer. Place the cans even with the ground around the plants they are foraging. Empty the disgusting can full of earwigs every few days.

Flies

Basil deters flies. Wipe down the tablecloth on your picnic table with an infusion of basil to keep flies away. Store the mixture in a spray bottle and use as needed.

Bothered by flies and other flying insects while barbequing? Lay rosemary or bay leaves over the coals. Not only will it deter the insects, it will also give the taste of your food a boost.

Garden Insects

Repel garden insects by planting the herbs mint, rosemary or sage.

Repel most insects by planting marigolds, asters, calendula, chrysanthemums, geraniums and onions.

Hyssop, rosemary, sage, mint and southernwood will deter the cabbage moth.

Celery, peppermint and wormwood deters the white cabbage butterfly.

Petunias will protect your bean crop.

Plant borage to improve the growth and flavor of your tomatoes. It will also deter the tomato worm.

Plant dead nettle to improve the growth and flavor of your potatoes. It will also deter the potato bug. Other deterrents are flax and horseradish.

Protect your cucumbers from the cucumber beetle by planting radishes.

Gophers

Repel gophers with daffodils.

Spray soil or plants with castor oil spray made from one tablespoon castor oil and one tablespoon liquid soap to one gallon of water.

Gophers are very sensitive to sound. Bury empty glass pop bottles halfway with the open end up. They will be scared off by the sound made when a breeze goes by.

Grubs

The best way to banish grubs is with milky spore disease, a natural occurring infection. It is sold in the form of a dust and is applied to the lawn. Do not apply it along with an insecticide as it kills the host for the disease and renders it useless.

Japanese Beetles

Plant garlic around the edge of your garden to repel Japanese beetles. The best time to plant garlic is September, October & November.

Plant garlic near your rosebushes to protect them from Japanese beetles.

Rue and white geranium plants will repel Japanese beetles. Other choices are forsythia, honeysuckle and privet.

Japanese beetles are attracted to larkspur and will kill them.

Moles

Repel moles by planting garlic around fruit & nut trees.

Moles feed on grubs – they can eat close to their own body weight every day! So get rid of the grubs, and the moles will be less likely to move in.

Soak a cotton ball with oil of peppermint, which can be purchased at health food stores. Drop the cotton ball down the mole hole. This remedy works for any rodent problem.

Mosquitoes

Put a lemon balm leaf in the campfire to deter mosquitoes.

Basil deters mosquitoes.

Make yourself less attractive to mosquitoes by eating less sugar because the people they really go for eat a lot of sugar.

Drink chamomile tea to repel mosquitoes.

If you have a pond or fountain in your yard, stock it with goldfish. They are wonderful for consuming mosquito larvae.

Moths

Moths are the adult version of many species of caterpillars and worm-like creatures – and they all do damage on top of being ugly. Interplant onion, garlic, tomato, tansy, celery, hyssop, mint, sage, rosemary or thyme – or try using them as border plants.

Cosmos works as a repellent for earworms.

Marigolds will repel tomato hornworms, and dill is a good trap crop for them.

Plant sunflowers as a good trap crop for many species of soon-to-be moths.

Use sweet clover in your clothes and linens to deter moths.

Dried chives also repel moths.

Repel moths with newspaper. Just put a layer of paper between the padding and the rug. This works because both insects hate printer's ink.

Nematodes

A nematode is an unsegmented worm. Sugar kills nematodes by causing them to dry up. 5 pounds of sugar to 100 pounds of soil will cause them to die off within 24 hours.

Pests

Plant wormwood as a border to keep animals from the garden.

Deter spiders with cotton balls sprayed with rubbing alcohol.

Try spreading some anise oil on your mousetraps as mice like the scent.

Keep snakes out of your flower garden by putting mothballs in the ground around the plants. This will also keep squirrels, dogs and cats away.

Rabbits

To keep rabbits out of your flower garden, mix 1 part talcum powder with 1 part hot pepper (capsicum) and sprinkle regularly over the area.

Deter rabbits by planting garlic, onions, chives, Mexican marigold or dusty miller near the plants they particularly like.

Sprinkle blood meal, onions, ground limestone or wood ashes around the edge of the garden to discourage rabbits.

Scatter dog hair around your plants – there is plenty of hair to be had from dog groomers.

Keep rabbits out of your garden by putting human hair in the feet of old pantyhose. Attach these to stakes around the garden's perimeter. When the rabbit gets a whiff, it will scare him off. Where to get the hair? Just ask your barber shop!

If all else fails – erect a fence!

Raccoons

Since raccoons love sweet corn, try dusting the leaves and ears with baby powder. That will keep them away.

Try spreading dog droppings in the rows of your garden to keep raccoons away.

Silverfish

Repel silverfish with newspaper. Just put a layer of paper between the padding and the rug. This works because both insects hate printer's ink.

Skunks

I had quite a problem with skunks a few years back, and they really made a mess out of my yard. The problems was that I had grubs – and skunks love grubs. Once I got rid of the grubs, the skunks left too.

Repel skunks with cloths soaked in ammonia.

Keep skunks away from digging a home under your deck or porch. Just hang a strong smelling bar of soap in the area, and it will repel the skunks.

Slugs

These disgusting looking creatures love dead leaves and decaying vegetation. To repel slugs, try interplanting rosemary or wormwood.

Make a wormwood tea and spray in on the ground in the fall to deter slugs. *Never use wormwood internally.*

Make a spray of two parts water to one part ammonia and spray on your hostas to prevent slugs.

Spread powdered ginger around your plants to keep slugs away.

Trap slugs with aluminum pie tins or empty tuna fish cans. Pour in about one inch of beer and then press the tin into the soil so it is even with the ground. You will soon be emptying out the dead slugs.

Put sharp sand around your hostas and clematis to deter slugs.

Catch slugs in orange or grapefruit rinds left face down in the soil.

Squirrels

Keep squirrels away from plants with a spray made from hot peppers. Puree about 4-5 hot peppers. Strain them, add 1-2 cups of water and 1 tablespoon liquid soap.

Have you ever seen a squirrel hanging from a squirrel-safe bird house? I have! The poles of the birdhouse were fed through PVC pipes strung on wires from the tree. These pipes would spin when the squirrels tried to walk across thus protecting the bird feeder. But the squirrel was smarter and simply jumped through the air, landing on the bird feeder and proceeded to knock the birdseed to the ground for his cohorts. You can prevent this by wrapping wide strips of metal flashing around the bottom to prevent the squirrel from getting a hold.

Keep squirrels out of your chimney by placing some moth crystals in an aluminum pie tin.

Insect Bites

Lemon Balm Oil is great for insect bites. As an ointment, it can be used to soothe insect bites or to repel insects.

Calendula salve, lotion, cream or oil soothes insect bites. It is gentle to the skin, even that of babies and the elderly.

For insect bites or infected sores, dissolve 10 drops of thyme oil in 20 drops of water and apply to the affected area.

To relieve the itch from insect bites, dab on some ammonia with a cotton swab.

Known mainly for its uses in the kitchen, parsley has medicinal qualities as well. It can be used as a poultice for insect bites.

The fresh leaves of the plantain plant will help a bee sting and wounds that are slow to heal when used as a poultice.

Mountain mint is an excellent insect repellent.

Try this natural insect repellent: Dilute 5 drops of basil oil in 10-ml. almond or sunflower oil and apply to the skin.

To deter mosquitoes and other biting insects, rub fresh

herbs on the skin of your arms and legs. Mountain mint, basil and lemongrass are especially effective. Or you can make an infusion of these herbs in sweet almond oil or witch hazel. Put the mixture in a spray bottle, and spray on your skin and clothes to repel the insects.

For Fleas:

Make an herbal flea powder by mixing 2 ounces pennyroyal and 1 ounce each of wormwood, rosemary and cayenne pepper. Store in a container and use as often as you would any other flea powder. Be sure to rub well into skin and avoid the eye area.

Lavender water will keep fleas off of you.

Try these aromatherapy oils: For dogs use essential oil of Juniper, Eucalyptus, Citronella, Geranium, Cedar or Lavender. For cats, use Lavender oil only or a prepared cat-safe combination. Put a few drops of the oil into a spray bottle of water and shake well before each use. Or you can rub the oil undiluted into a rope collar as a repellent renewing the oil weekly.

Add oil of lavender to pets bedding. It will deter the fleas as well as help to make the bedding smell sweet.

Flea collars have lots of poison in them. How many times have you touched one and then touched food, or put your hand to your mouth before washing your hands? You might be careful, but this is a danger to children.

Make your own natural flea collar by combining oil of citrus, oil of lavender (both can be purchased at your local health food store) with slices of lemon and some water. Soak an ordinary pet collar in this material overnight and let dry before fastening around your pet's neck.

Chapter 8:

Amish Cooking

...In the summertime there was a lot of canning, and we had our own fruit. I'd go help pick the fruit and then can it so there was a lot of work like that. After the fruit and the vegetables were harvested, canning began in June with the strawberries. Now I freeze them but mom always canned hers. We would pick the fruit and can as the fruit was harvested. Canning season lasts until right around Christmas time usually or into January when the hogs get butchered. We always butchered our own hogs, beef and chickens. That would give us a couple of months usually to do quilting or sewing before it was time to start with the gardening again. So every month had its own thing. And it still does only we don't raise our own beef and we don't use pork. We don't raise chickens anymore either. I wanted to because I was used to them, but my husband didn't care for them so we never raised our own chickens...

Laura's Fruit Dessert

...I use a big can of Dole pineapple juice. I heat that and thicken it with Fricheggs. You can buy this at an Amish store. It is used to thicken similar to corn starch but you can put the leftover in the freezer. I use all fructose, I do not use sugar. If I just want to use it with can fruit I would put a little bit of fructose in there my thickener. Then I drain the fruit and mix some pineapple, peaches maybe some cherries, and this pineapple juice and eat it plain...

Mom's Pie Crust

3 cups flour	1 egg
1 tsp salt	1 TBL white vinegar
1 1/4 cup shortening	4 TBL water

Mix together the flour, salt and shortening and set aside. Mix together one beaten egg with the vinegar and water. Add to flour, mix until mixture holds together. Place on floured surface and roll. Makes one 9˝ pie shell. Bake at 350 degrees for 15 minutes.

Custard Pie

1/3 cup sugar
1/2 tsp salt
3 cups milk
1/4 tsp cinnamon

2 tsp flour
3 eggs
1/4 tsp nutmeg

Combine sugar, flour, salt and eggs and mix well. Heat milk to boiling. Add one cup hot milk to the egg mixture then pour that mixture into the remaining hot milk. Pour into unbaked 9" pie shell and sprinkle nutmeg and cinnamon on the top. Bake at 350 degrees for 40-45 minutes.

Easy Apple Butter

8 quarts chunky applesauce
4 cups brown sugar
dash of vanilla

8 quarts fresh apple cider
1 tsp salt

Place hot applesauce in a roaster into the oven at 400 degrees. Place cider in large stockpot on top of the stove and bring to a boil. Let it continue to boil until half of it has evaporated. Then add it to the applesauce in the oven. Leave the oven door ajar and stir occasionally for two hours. Then add the sugar, salt and vanilla and mix well. Continue to cook and stir occasionally for two additional hours until apple butter is the desired consistency. Seal into prepared jars.

Dill Pickles

Cucumbers, wash & pat dry
Garlic
Fresh Dill
4 1/4 cups apple cider vinegar
4 cups water

Onions
Pickling spice
1 1/4 cups sugar
1/2 cup coarse salt

Into each prepared quart jar place 2 heads fresh dill, one small onion, one clove of garlic and 1/2 teaspoon pickling spice. Pack prepared cucumbers, either whole or sliced, into each jar. In a large saucepan combine sugar, vinegar, salt and water. Heat to boiling. Pour over cucumbers in each jar and immediately put on the lids. Place the filled jars in water and bring the water to a full boil. Turn off the heat and let jars sit in the hot water for 5 minutes before removing. Seal each jar.

...At Christmas time Mom always made huge batches of candy. So that meant she would cook centers one day for the O'Henry® bars for the chocolate drops everything. She would do those one day, get those ready. Then the next day we would be dipping candy all day long, make peanut brittle, whatever. I can't see why we weren't sick. The holiday meal we would have mashed potatoes and stuffing both. We hardly ever had a turkey, we mostly had chicken. That was usually cut up and fixed the regular way. There was just more food. We didn't have different foods just more of it. Mom always fried her chicken. I don't, I bake...

Laura's Fiesta Chicken

...Take one pound cubed chicken breast. Brown in skillet and add salt and pepper. Add two cans cream of mushroom soup, 3 teaspoons chili powder, one medium onion, one sweet pepper – it can be any color, red, green or yellow and one large tomato chopped. Add this to the soup, then to chicken. Add one half bag crushed tortilla chips, the most natural you can find. Put half of the mixture in the bottom of a large casserole and cover with two cups of shredded cheddar cheese. Add another layer of the mixture and end with the cheese. Bake covered at 350 degrees for one hour. The corn chips make it taste like it has corn in it...

Holiday Chicken

2 cups Townhouse® or Ritz® cracker crumbs
2 cups flour   2 TBL paprika
1 TBL sugar   1 1/2 tsp black pepper
2 tsp garlic powder   2 tsp garlic salt
2 tsp celery salt

Soak chicken pieces in salt water overnight. Drain and pat dry. Crush crackers and mix with remaining ingredients. Roll chicken in crumbs then fry in skillet in olive oil and butter till browned. Transfer pieces to roaster and cover lightly. Bake at 350 for 1 hour.

... Oh the things they fed us, sometimes when we think back at what we ate bowls and bowls of, we just get over it. She would fix fried potatoes and sausage and instead of a vegetable we would have custard pudding. I just can't

imagine that because the potatoes were always so greasy and the sausage and then this custard pudding to go along with it. But we ate bowls of it all together. Another meal in the summertime was a huge bowl of red potatoes and just as big a bowl of cabbage that was shredded and creamed. Hardly anybody does it that way. Mom would shred it and cook it with butter and probably cream because she always had the cream off the milk and a thickening of milk and flour and then salt and pepper added to it. It was delicious. It goes very good with the red potatoes. But my family doesn't agree with me so I don't make it anymore....

Vegetable Salad

1 bunch fresh broccoli	2 cups shredded cheddar cheese
1 head fresh cauliflower	1 pkg bacon, cooked & diced
Dressing:	
1 1/2 cups sour cream	1 1/2 cups Miracle Whip® salad dressing
1 cup sugar	2 pks Hidden Valley Ranch® dressing powder

Combine dressing ingredients to vegetables. Mix and serve.

Laura's Brown Rice

...Brown rice is good for the heart. Every morning I mix wild rice and brown rice and add water. It has to simmer for one to one and a half hours. I like to do that. That's my thing to put on the stove and go for the garden and know I can come back in and it's done itself where potatoes would burn. We don't use that much pasta...

Laura's Beef Stew

...I was going to have Beef stew for lunch. Then add the brown rice, carrots, onion, green beans. The rice takes care of the gravy...

Granola

6 cups quick cook oats
3/4 cups sliced almonds
1 cup raisins
3 TBL water
1/2 cup honey
1 1/2 tsp maple extract

1/2 cup wheat bran
1/2 cup coconut
3/4 cup olive oil
1/2 cup brown sugar
1 1/2 tsp vanilla

In a large bowl mix together the oats, wheat bran, almonds, coconut and raisins. In a saucepan combine the remaining ingredients. Stir over low heat till combined and just warm. Pour over dry ingredients until coated. Pour into baking dish and bake at 275 degrees for approximately one hour stirring every 15 minutes. Do not overbrown. Cool, then store in sealed container.

... In a traditional meal we always had vegetables and usually potatoes or stuffing, one or the other, never both except on holidays. Always meat. The evening meal we always had homemade soup. We grew up on soup, all different kinds. Dessert was usually a fruit and probably cookies or a cake all from scratch. I can't stand the smell of store bought cake mixes. It reminds me of the smell of milk replacer. Later on we used to mix milk replacer to feed the calfs. That's what you used to feed the calf instead of milk. It was a powder we mixed with water and attached to a great big nipple to feed the calfs. When I would mix the powder it always blew up into my nose. The smell of the cake mixes as the powder goes up in your face reminds me of that milk replacer. I can even smell it in the cakes. I don't care for it, I can't eat them....

Chicken Broth

In large stock pot combine one cut up fryer, one whole onion, one whole carrot, one whole tomato, one whole stalk of celery, one garlic clove and a handful of black peppercorns. Fill with water and simmer on the stove until chicken is done. Strain. When cool break chicken into small pieces and either put back into broth or freeze separately for later use. Add a handful of romano cheese and salt to taste. Put some broth into ice cube trays and freeze for later use during cooking. The remaining broth can be frozen or used immediately.

Rivvel Soup

4 cups chicken broth
1 cup flour
pinch black pepper

1 beaten egg
1/2 tsp salt

Bring chicken broth to a boil. Combine flour, salt, pepper and egg with hands until they form soft lumps. Drop these into the boiling broth and simmer for 15 minutes. Add additional cooked vegetables if desired and simmer 5 more minutes.

Amish Peanut Butter Spread

3 cups brown sugar
1 3/4 cups water

1 cup peanut butter
2 cups marshmallow cream

Make a syrup with the water and brown sugar by bringing to a boil in a small saucepan. Let cool. Mix the peanut butter and marshmallow cream together and slowly begin adding the syrup until the desired consistency is reached. Does not need refrigerated.

Meadow Tea

2 cups sugar
2 lemons
2 cups fresh peppermint or spearmint leaves

1 quart water
additional water

Combine sugar and 1 quart water in a saucepan and bring to a boil. Pour over leaves and let steep for 20 minutes. Remove the leaves and cool. Squeeze the juice from the lemons into the tea and add water to make one gallon. Serve or warm or cold.

Chapter 9:

Laura's Remembrances and More!

In the hills and valleys of what we call Amish Country, the clothes lines filled with the laundry of plain clothes flaps in the soft breeze. Road signs give a warning to drivers to share the road with the plentiful horse and buggies.

...When I was growing up, we did a huge laundry, but only on Mondays. Now I do the laundry two or three days a week...

Laziness does not exist here. Farming is the common occupation, both poultry farms for chickens and dairy farms for milk and cheese. But Amish men and women also work as a blacksmith, seamstress and carpenter. They work in bakeries, bulk food stores, book stores, cabinet shops, engine repair shops, greenhouses, harness shops, buggy repair shops and provide services like tool sharpening, upholstery repair or watch and clock repair. There are manufacturing operations and factories owned and operated by Amish that produce products like farm equipment, sawmills, buggies and furniture. Mobile work crews in carpentry, wood working, home construction and interior redecorating are in demand for the high quality work they produce.

Tourism is huge in Amish settlements and many single Amish women work in the restaurants and hotels. Many Amish farms open up their property to tours. Some private Amish homes actually open up their homes to busloads of strangers and serve authentic made-from-scratch Amish meals right on the premises for as many as 200 people a day.

Some families build a separate building near the main house in order to handle larger groups of people. The seating is normally at long tables placed end to end, and the food is served family style. Hearty, comfort food weigh down the platters of the typical Amish fare. The heavenly aromas of baked chicken, pot roast, ham, mashed potatoes, vegetables and fresh baked breads fill the air. Homemade apple butter and peanut butter spread are a common accompaniment as well as plentiful pies and cakes.

Often there are fundraisers in the form of auctions. Featured at these auctions are the beautiful handmade quilts for which the Amish are so well known.

... When I was a girl we went to bed between 9PM and midnight. It depended on the book I had to read, we were bookworms. The gas lights were always on and we would read a book every night. Some families played games or crocheted or embroidered. I would crochet. I make place mats out of nylon from Haiti. The Haitian men do this over there. Mom used to piece quilts in the evening. Most of them at that time were for the children. We had ten children in our family and we all got quilts. The five boys got three quilts and the girls got four. So that was a lot of quilting. We still try to quilt now for benefits and church raffles not so much for the family....

The Amish are like the quilts they make, each patch may be different, but the Amish as a community of people are sewn together by their common history and religious values.

... Mom would make our clothes with fabric she'd buy at the fabric store. When they would wear out, she would make carpet rags. Right now I have boxes and boxes of knit skirts in the attic. I should cut them into small strips and make braided rugs. They're bulky and would last forever. Maybe I could sell them. I should do that but when do I ever had the time? I was thinking I could crochet them so I bought great big hooks, but I never got around to it....

Free time in an Amish community may include barn raising to help one of their own. Women gather leaves of mint for meadow tea to serve along with the hearty homemade meal for all the workers.

Often times the women get together and make gallons and gallons of vegetable soup and other foods to be divided up and frozen for winter use. This is a good idea that we can use in our own lives. Get a group of friends together and once a month have a cooking party. Divide and freeze the final result for that week's meals or for later use. It's also a good way to keep in touch. This can be done with canning and baking as well.

Besides the cooking and other chores that take place on an Amish homestead, there are recreational activities as well. In the wintertime there may be skating on the pond. During the summer months they enjoy baseball and fishing although never on Sunday as that is taboo. There are shuffleboard competitions and picnics by the creek. The Amish believe that fun activities not only build useful skills but also a sense of well being.

Besides worship, Sundays was a time for visiting. A person who does a lot of visiting is well liked and it shows concern for your family and friends.

...We did a lot of visiting. My dad was a deacon when we were a little bit older and they would always go off to church. That was kind of when it stopped that we didn't go visiting so much. We have church every other Sunday. On the in between Sunday we would go visit other churches or go visit family...

Laura has not had an easy time of it. Her husband had open heart surgery, and she herself has had some health problems. Laura believes in the healing power of magnets along with a wholesome diet of natural foods and daily exercise. Here's her story in her own words...

...My husband had open heart surgery in December. His blood pressure is still high. When he uses the medication everything just dries out so bad. He said "Well I still have a dry mouth, is that still coming from that?" I said "Sure! It's still a side effect from your medication." Our family doctor explained this on Thursday night to him. He said what the doctors do with the medication is dry your system out. The vessels have to be elastic and move. So you have to hydrate your body until those are elastic then your blood pressure will be normal. So it's hydration. We're really working on that...

...I was very ill. I had two herniated disks, and my back hurt. My neighbor took me into her room and showed me the mattress pad and pillow she had. She told me to sit down on them and try them out. My body is very sensitive, and I knew I would know right away if it would help me so I sat down. Instantly I felt a tingling that went from my tailbone and down my left leg. She also let me use her handheld magnets. I was holding them on my back and the tingling went up my arms into my neck and up into head. So I took them home for the

evening. She said just massage where it hurts. Well I hurt all over. I went to bed and I slept better that night than I had in a long time. The next morning after getting the breakfast and doing the dishes, which that was a job, I was able to do laundry. My husband helped me use my laundry cart to take it and get started. So I did the laundry and hung it outside on the line. The girls, all three came home and said "Mom, did Dad put the laundry on the line for you?" I said "Nope, I did. But go get it." So that was the start. From day one I could do a half day of work. Before that I was in there on the recliner crocheting. I would fix meals. And if I fixed too much of a meal I could not mash a potato or cook gravy because that would irritate my back. I just can't get over it. For 17 years I was that way. It's been 10 years now and every year I feel better...

...This winter I've had to back off. I've had a heart problem for 21 years and nobody did an EKG so I didn't know what it was. My neighbor told me what her symptoms were, but the symptoms are different with everyone. She told me about the acid reflux and the pressure in the ears, the jaws the neck. Being a nurse she said she should have known what was going on. But she went to the hospital thinking it was acid reflux and ended up with two stints. So I came in and told my husband, she just described all these symptoms I've had for years. So I went to have it checked out. The day I had the EKG, it was like pins and needles all through my body. After that it was just worse. I ended up having a stress test. Just by dilating the vessels it broke through the blockage or whatever it was. So it was my heart. And I'm not on any medicine...

...I drink juice, a dietary supplement, every day. The juice I drink contains red pomegranates, brown rice and other good things. I drink one ounce every day. Another thing I do is drink a fruit and vegetable juice together in the morning. By doing this you have eight times the antioxidants fighting for you than if you just took the fruit or vegetables alone. Before, my stomach hurt but it ended up it was my heart. I'm so sensitive that the first time I drank the juice I just felt a burning sensation. I couldn't do much. Oh I did what I had to do but not any more because I just didn't feel like it. It's been six weeks. Down the road is a big hill and last week I decided to just give myself my own stress test. I just walked up that hill and back, I think I could have given a horse a race, and it didn't hurt. In those six weeks of the whole foods, it has really done wonders...

Chapter 10:

Eye Catching Gardens

Butterfly Garden

My mother-in-law has the most beautiful butterfly garden I've ever seen. The path twists and turns as you walk atop the garden stones she carefully laid. A lovely bench sits right in the middle of the garden. She enjoys sitting there reading and watching the delightful fluttering.

Creating your own butterfly habitat doesn't take a lot of work. Choose the spot that is away from the wind and captures the early morning sunlight. This is important because butterflies must raise their body temperature to between 86 and 104 degrees F. to be able to fly at all. Once their little bodies have been warmed by the morning sun, you can get ready to be enchanted.

You need to purchase a butterfly house One thing that my mother-in-law did was to place a twig near the entrance that was rather *nubby* as she called it. They like to cling to this as they go into the butterfly house. You also need to place a flat dish of water near the house so the butterflies can get a drink. Be sure the dish doesn't have much depth to it.

Some suggestions for plants that will attract the butterflies are: Pink coneflower, butterfly bush, bee balm, flowering tobacco (Nicotiana), sweet William, snapdragon, cosmos, Pampas, Gooseneck and Zebra grasses. They really do like to flutter around the ornamental grasses. Be sure to plant some Parsley near the butterfly house – they especially love it.

Scientists have proven that butterflies can identify colors. Their favorites are purple, pink, yellow and white so keep these in mind when planning your garden.

Special Tip: Sprinkle a few banana peels and orange peels around to attract the butterflies in.

Your butterfly garden won't develop overnight. Have

patience and enjoy it.

Flower Garden

Pretty flowers make us smile. They are pleasing to the eye and add a pleasing appearance to your home. The color of the flowers you plant reflect the personality of your home. Warm colors like yellow, orange and red make a flower garden appear smaller attract attention to the area where they are planted. Cool colors like blue and purple make the garden seem larger and create a sense of tranquility.

Flowers are natures way of scenting the earth. When choosing the flowers for your garden, don't just go for color – go for fragrance. If you're not sure, look for bulb packages that are marked fragrant.

What is considered to be a pleasing scent? The answer will vary from person to person Different varieties of the same flowers can have different *fragrances.*

For example: *Hyacinths* can be exotic, spicy or sweet-smelling.
Narcissus can smell like vanilla, jasmine or musk.
Tulips can be sweet, fruity or delicate.

Whether you like the heady aroma of daffodils or the soft fragrance of lavender, do some experimenting and come up with what pleases *you.*

The best time to plant flower bulbs is in the fall. Dig a hole about 6 inches deep and add a little of your compost material and some bulb fertilizer. Hardy bulbs like tulips should be planted all together instead of one at a time. Be sure to place the bulbs in the bottom of the hole with the tips up. Cover with good soil and water gently to soak all the way down. Protect your flower bed for the winter with mulch.

Annuals are plants that grow, flower, set seed and die within the same season. *Biennials* will live for two seasons. *Perennials* will continue to grow for at least three seasons in the same location. Keep this in mind when planning your flower garden.

Flower name	Color	Size	Sun/Shade
Uses	When to plant	Expect Blooms	
Chrysanthemum	Red, white, yellow	1-2 feet	Sun
Borders, Vases	Early spring	July	
Bachelor's Button	Blue, pink, white	1-1 1/2 feet	Sun
Arrangements	September	April	
Snapdragon	Variety	1-3 feet	Sun
Borders, beds, vases	January indoors	Early summer	
Moonflower	White	6 feet	Night flowering
Beds	Early Spring	Summer (But I never planted mine!)	
Sunflower	Yellow	2-10 feet	Sun, partial shade
Birds love it	Spring	Late summer & fall	
Baby's Breath	White	Up to 1 foot	Sun
Beds	Spring	Summer	
Larkspur	Blue, pinks	3-4 feet	Sun
Beds, borders	March, April	July, August	
Lobelia	Blues, white	4-10 feet	Light
shade			
Borders, flower boxes	February indoors	Spring	
Nicotiana	Pink, red, white	3 feet	Sun, partial shade
Butterfly garden	Spring	Mid-summer	
Petunia	Pinks, purples, red, white	1-1 1/2 feet	Sun
Beds, borders	March indoors	Summer, fall	
Black-eyed Susan	Beige, orange, yellow with purple center	6 feet	Partial shade
Vine	Spring	Mid-summer to fall	
Marigolds	Orange, yellow	6 inches-4 feet	Sun
Beds, borders	Spring	Summer	
Zinnia	Orange, pinks, purple, red, yellow	1-1 1/2 feet	Sun
Beds, borders	Spring	Summer	

Color in your Herb Garden

Everyone uses color in different ways. But there is a standard correlation to the color of the herb and what it signifies:

Dark blue	Joy
Light blue	Peace, tranquility, inspiration
Green	Prosperity, fertility
White	Purity, healing
Yellow	Healing
Gold	Luck, success
Orange	Healing
Brown	Money
Pink	Friendship, love
Red	Love, passion, courage

Create a beautiful display of color with your herb garden!

Plant blues such as sage, rosemary, chicory, love-in-a-mist, pansies, larkspur, blue flag, hyssop, rue or borage.

Use yellow plants such as nasturtium, witch hazel, tansy, goldenrod, St. John's wort, dill, tansy, calendula, evening primrose, lady's mantle or yarrow.

Go with purples such as lavender, violets, oregano, saffron or peppermint.

Add some whites such as angelica, chamomile, feverfew, Lily-of-the-valley or sweet basil.

Use red plants such as bergamot, hollyhock, cardinal flower or crimson thyme.

Try pinks such as fenugreek, English pennyroyal, or foxglove. Or for a more dramatic center, use orange such as calendula, coltsfoot or butterfly weed.

Silver herbs such as Lamb's ears, silver sage, silver thyme and silver beacon add a touch of sparkle.

Chapter 11:

Garden Remedies From Readers

The National Garden Bureau claims that gardeners cope better with stress and tension. This could be because the tasks of preparing the soil, planting, weeding and harvesting are great releases for pent-up emotions.

It is a proven fact that the ability to vent your frustrations and cope with stress is a key factor in achieving and maintaining good health. So, head for the garden to stay healthy, live longer and be happy!

I used to own a car wash. An easy way I found to clean the cushions from the patio furniture was to take them to the car wash with me. I scrubbed them with a brush and some good heavy-duty cleaner then just rinsed them off...

Pete S.

... "My daughter got gum in her beautiful long hair. It was so bad, I thought I was going to have to cut it. But my mother-in-law came to the rescue with egg whites. It was a yucky, slimy mess but it worked...

Mary S.

"...Use manure while planting. Just put it around the young plants with water to help them grow better..."

Victor D.

...To make sure there are no bugs in head of cabbage, I always would soak them in cold water with about a tablespoon of white vinegar added...

Jo D.

...I use old pantyhose that have runners in them lots of ways. One thing I do is hang a pair outside by the garden hose. I put small slivers of soap in the toe and use it to wash up – right through the hose. This is handy for use after gardening, working on the car or any outside chores. As a bar of soap gets too small to use inside, I add the pieces to my hose bag...

Natalie B.

...My aunt always had beautiful fern plants. Her secret was she put a layer of coffee grounds on top of the dirt...

Harry S.

"...I used to dry my flower bouquets from school dances with laundry detergent. Just cover the flowers completely in dry detergent. 2 weeks later you will have dried flowers..."

Mary S.

"...Don't put grass clippings around your plants – they make a bed for the bugs..."

Victor D.

"...I never used fertilizer or pesticide on my garden. I had an organic garden. I used apple cores, potato peelings and stuff from the table. I would munch the leaves with the mower and spread it over the garden to sweeten the ground. When it rots, I turn it over with my rototiller..."

Victor D.

"...I water my houseplants with vinegar and water. Just add about 1 tablespoon to every gallon of water. My friends think I really have a green thumb!..."

David W.

"...My sister-in-law always used flavored gelatin to feed her plants. She used 4 quarts of water for every small box of gelatin. I can't say I tried it myself, but her plants always did great..."

Jo D.

...Keep rabbits out of your garden and away from your cabbage and lettuce by sprinkling cayenne pepper right onto the leaves. Nothing else I ever tried seemed to work but this. You have to repeat this after every time it rains...

Mike H.

"...My trees were always the healthiest looking trees on the block. When I sat down to have a beer, I gave my tree one too. Just pour it on the ground around the base of the tree..."

Pete S.

... Whenever my girls got grass-stained knees, I would just put plain rubbing alcohol on it, rub it together and wash as usual. They always came clean...

Ann H.

"...I use vinegar to keep my cat away from places I don't want her near. I keep it in a spray bottle and use it on furniture and my plant stands..."

David W.

"...Put moth balls in holes and around the area you see little chipmunks..."

Mike H.

"...Be sure to pull the suckers from your tomato plants. If you don't you'll have one big bush and no big tomatoes. By pulling the suckers you'll have less tomatoes but they'll be big and plump..."

Victor D.

"... My dad used to wrap green tomatoes in newspaper and keep them in the garage until winter. Can you believe those tomatoes got ripe?!"...

Norma S.

"...To keep ants away just break up pieces of eggshell and put it near their entry to your house. They hate it and will soon leave. This hint works even better if you know where the nest is outside..."

Jo D.

...I used to protect my small plants from frost with empty plastic milk gallons. Cover the plant then just push them down into the dirt about three inches or so...

Pete S.

"...I enjoy a cup of chamomile tea now and then. When I have some, I also share it with my young plants. It seems to help them grow stronger..."

David W.

"...Spread some baking soda around your tomato plants to make them taste sweeter..."

Rod W.

"...I kept my cat away from my flowers by putting the screen from my old windows all around the garden and covering them with dirt. It took a couple of times for her to get her claws stuck and she never went back..."

Natalie B.

"...I always cleaned my fresh heads of cauliflower by soaking the head in ice water. Just keep the stem side up and it will remove any bugs..."

Jo D.

"...Stretch a garden hose around your garden to keep out rabbits. They think it is a snake..."

Mike H.

"...I always freeze whole tomatoes to use when I make homemade soup. Just put the whole tomato in to add color and flavor to the broth..."

Josephine D.

"...Plants like to hear soft music. It seems to perk them up to grow a little faster and taller. Ordinary plants that are abandoned are droopy..."

Victor D.

"...I always talked to the plants in my garden. I would say *Grow little plant, grow and bear fruit.* When they got bigger I would tell them *Now you're on your own. I've helped you all I can...*"

Victor D.

"...For nice and white heads of cauliflower, wrap the leaves around the head to protect it from the sun ..."

Rod W.

I've thoroughly enjoyed working on this project and feel more than just a little sadness as it comes to an end. But I am always getting suggestions and tips for more and more gardening remedies. I'll bet you have some of your own ideas, hints and wonderful potions that you could share with me and my readers. I would love to hear from you! Please use the form on page 109.

Marcy D. Nicholas

Thank You

Thank you so much for purchasing *"Amish Gardening Secrets"*.

If you have a personal experience that you would like to share, some special advice or ideas and comments about this book, I would love to hear from you! If I can use it in a future edition, I will gladly send you a free copy of the new book.

My sincere thanks, and to you I extend my wishes for the best of everything.

Marcy

_____

_____

_____

_____

Please indicate (yes or no) whether I may use your name if I use your helpful advice:

YES, please give credit to _____
(Please print)

NO, please use my advice, but do not use my name in the book

(Either way, Yes or No, if I use your advice or personal experience, I'll send you a free copy of the new edition.)

Reorder Form

90-Day Money-Back Guarantee

❏ YES. Please rush _____ additional copies of *"Amish Gardening Secrets"* and my FREE copy of the bonus booklet *"Anti Aging Tips"* for only $9.95 plus $3.98 postage & handling. I understand that I must be completely satisfied or can return it within 90 days for a full and prompt refund of my purchase price. The FREE gift is mine to keep regardless. *Want to save even more?* Do a favor for a relative or close friend and order a second book. That's 2 for only $20 postpaid.

Amish Gardening Secrets

VISA DISCOVER MasterCard AMEX

I am enclosing $_____ by: ❏ Check ❏ Money Order (Make checks payable to James Direct Inc)

Charge my credit card Signature _____

Card No. _____ Exp. date _____

Name _____

Address _____

City _____ State _____ Zip _____

❏ Yes! I'd like to know about freebies, specials and new products before they are nationally advertised. My email address is: _____

Mail To: **JAMES DIRECT INC. • PO Box 980, Dept. GB294 Hartville, Ohio 44632**
http://www.jamesdirect.com

Use this coupon to order *"Amish Gardening Secrets"* for a friend or family member -- or co
the ordering information onto a plain piece of paper and mail to:

Amish Gardening Secrets
Dept. GB294
PO Box 980
Hartville, Ohio 44632

Preferred Customer Reorder Form

rder this...	If you want a book on...	Cost...	Number of Copies...
Amish Gardening Secrets	You too can learn the special gardening secrets the Amish use to produce huge tomato plants and bountiful harvests. Information packed 800-plus collection for you to tinker with and enjoy.	$9.95	
Garlic: ture's Natural Companion	Exciting scientific research on garlic's ability to promote good health. Find out for yourself why garlic has the reputation of being able to heal almost magically! Newest in Emily's series of natural heath books!	$9.95	
gelwhispers: ten for them in your life	The coincidences that happen in our lives, the little nudges in our minds... that is our angels! Learn to recognize the *Angelwhispers* in your daily life for joy, blessings and abundance.	$9.95	
Emily's aster Guide of Natural Remedies	Emily's new guide to infectious diseases & their threat on our health. What happens if we can't get to the pharmacy – or the shelves are empty, *what then*? What if the electricity goes out – and stays out? What if my neighborhood was quarantined? How would I feed my family? Handle first aid? 208 page book!	$9.95	
he Vinegar ome Guide	Learn how to clean and freshen with natural, environmentally-safe vinegar in the house, garden and laundry. Plus, delicious home-style recipes!	$9.95	

✓ combination of the above $9.95 items qualifies for following discounts...

Total NUMBER of $9.95 items

rder any 2 items for: $15.95	Order any 4 items for: $24.95	Order any 6 items for: $34.95 and receive 7th item	FREE Any additional items for: $5 each
rder any 3 items for: $19.95	Order any 5 items for: $29.95		

FEATURED SELECTIONS

Total COST of $9.95 items

The Magic of Baking Soda	*Plain Old Baking Soda A Drugstore in A Box?* Doctors & researchers have discovered baking soda has amazing healing properties! Over 600 health & Household Hints. *Great Recipes Too!*	$12.95	
The Honey Book	Amazing Honey Remedies to relieve arthritis pain, kill germs, heal infection and much more!	$19.95	
The Magic of drogen Peroxide	An Ounce of Hydrogen Peroxide is worth a Pound of Cure! Hundreds of health cures, household uses & home remedy uses for hydrogen peroxide contained in this breakthrough volume.	$19.95	
The Vinegar nniversary Book	Completely updated with the latest research and brand new remedies and uses for apple cider vinegar. Handsome coffee table collector's edition you'll be proud to display. *Big 208-page book!*	$19.95	

der any 2 or more Featured Selections for only $10 each...	Postage & Handling	$3.98*
	TOTAL	

* Shipping of 10 or more books = $6.96

90-DAY MONEY-BACK GUARANTEE

Please rush me the items marked above. I understand that I must be completely satisfied or I can return any item within 90 days with proof of purchase for a full and prompt refund of my purchase price.

I am enclosing $_____ by: ❑ Check ❑ Money Order (Make checks payable to James Direct Inc)

Charge my credit card Signature _____

VISA MasterCard DISCOVER AMEX

Card No. _____ Exp. Date _____

Name _____ Address _____

City _____ State _____ Zip _____

Telephone Number (_____) _____

❑ Yes! I'd like to know about freebies, specials and new products before they are nationally advertised. My em
address is: _____

Mail To: **James Direct Inc.** • PO Box 980, Dept. A1193 • Hartville, Ohio 44632
Customer Service (330) 877-0800 • *http://www.jamesdirect.com*

013 JDI A204IM

AMISH GARDENING SECRETS

There's something for everyone in *Amish Gardening Secrets*. This BIG collection contains over 800 gardening hints, suggestions, time savers and tonics that have been passed down over the years in Amish communities and elsewhere.

- -

GARLIC: NATURE'S NATURAL COMPANION

Explore the very latest studies and new remedies using garlic to help with cholesterol, blood pressure, asthma, arthritis, digestive disorders, bacteria, cold and flu symptoms, and MUCH MORE! Amazing cancer studies!

- -

ANGELWHISPERS: *Listen for them in your life*

Do you Believe in Angels? Angels are ready to help us in lots of ways. They can protect us from danger, reduce our fears, pain, worries and even help us find ways to cope with our problems. Learn the techniques in this book to improve every aspect of your life – *even your wealth!*

- -

EMILY'S DISASTER GUIDE OF NATURAL REMEDIES

Emily's most important book yet! If large groups of the population become sick at the same time, the medical services in this country will become stressed to capacity. *What then'* We will all need to know what to do! Over 307 natural cures, preventatives, cure-alls and ways to prepare to naturally treat & prevent infectious disease.

- -

THE VINEGAR HOME GUIDE

Emily Thacker presents her second volume of hundreds of all-new vinegar tips. Use versatile vinegar to add a low-sodium zap of flavor to your cooking, as well as getting your house "white-glove" clean for just pennies. Plus, safe and easy tips on shining and polishing brass, copper & pewter and removing stubborn stains & static cling in your laundry!

- -

THE MAGIC OF BAKING SODA

We all know baking soda works like magic around the house. It cleans, deodorizes & works wonders in the kitchen and in the garden. But did you know it's an effective remedy for allergies, bladder infection, heart disorders... *and MORE!*

- -

THE HONEY BOOK

Each page is packed with healing home remedies and ways to use honey to heal wounds, fight tooth decay, treat burns, fight fatigue, restore energy, ease coughs and even make cancer-fighting drugs more effective. Great recipes too!

- -

THE MAGIC OF HYDROGEN PEROXIDE

Hundreds of health cures & home remedy uses for hydrogen peroxide. You'll be amazed to see how a little hydrogen peroxide mixed with a pinch of this or that from your cupboard can do everything from relieving chronic pain to making age spots go away! Easy household cleaning formulas too!

- -

THE VINEGAR ANNIVERSARY BOOK

Handsome coffee table edition and brand new information on Mother Nature's Secret on – apple cider vinegar!

's own FREE Bonus!